Band Director Foundations For Success

William Clayton Miller

Major N. Alan Clark Ph.D. USAF (ret)

Copyright © 2014 Catherine McNamara

All rights reserved.

ISBN: 0692338357

ISBN-13: 978-0692338353

Table of Contents

PREFACE TO THE SECOND EDITION BY CATHERINE MCNAMARA 10

PREFACE TO THE SECOND EDITION BY N. ALAN CLARK 12

PREFACE TO THE FIRST EDITION BY WILLIAM CLAYTON MILLER 13

PART 1: PHILOSOPHICAL UNDERPINNINGS

CHAPTER 1: IDEALS AND MENTORSHIP 20
- **REKINDLING THE CULTURE OF MENTORSHIP** 21
- RECRUITING AND BUILDING A STRONG BEGINNING BAND PROGRAM 23
- REHEARSALS 24
- ADMINISTRATION OF THE BAND AND THE BAND BOOSTER ORGANIZATION 25

CHAPTER 2: EXPECTATION LEVEL 26

CHAPTER 3: BANDSMAN ATTITUDE AND MOTIVATION 30
- THE BAND DIRECTOR'S BRAIN BANK 30
- THE PYRAMID OF SUCCESS 30
- A WINNING TEACHING PHILOSOPHY 31

PART 2: TONE, TUNING AND ARTICULATION

CHAPTER 4: PROPER EMBOUCHURE FOCUS 36
- SONORITY 37
- MATURE TONE 37
- GOOD INTONATION 38
- GOOD BALANCE 38
- VOCABULARY 38
- THE EMBOUCHURE FOCUS 39
- PLAYERS MUST BE TAUGHT 40
- TRAINING ENSEMBLES FOR FINE SONORITY 41
- SPECIFICS CONCERNING PROPER EMBOUCHURE FOCUS 41
- TONGUE POSITION 44
- CORRECTING THE PINCHED EMBOUCHURE 45
- STAMINA DEVELOPMENT FOR THE WIND PLAYER 46
- TONE DRIVES 48
- THE "SQUEEZE PLAY" 49
- ENDURANCE 50
- DYNAMICS 51
- ACCURACY 51

Range	51
Intonation Deficiencies of Wind Instruments	52
Review	52
Solos	54

CHAPTER 5: BUZZING ... 56
The "Sing, Buzz, Blow" Technique	57
Sing	57
Buzz	57
Blow	57
Buzz the Music	58
Woodwinds	58

CHAPTER 6: DWELLING ... 60

CHAPTER 7: PROJECTION AND THE PERFORMANCE ENVIRONMENT ... 62
Improving Your Perspective with the Help of a Colleague	62

CHAPTER 8: STEP-UP MOUTHPIECES ... 64
Mouthpiece Recommendations:	64

CHAPTER 9: NILO HOVEY CLINIC: TUNING THE CLARINET AND THE BAND ... 66
The Clinic	66
Cross Tuning	69
Dealing with Certain Notes	70
The Mystery of the Squeaking Clarinets, Part One	72

CHAPTER 10: A ROUTINE FOR TUNING THE BAND ... 74
A Tuning Philosophy	74
Definition of Concert Pitch	75
Electronic Tuners	76
Wind Instruments Are Not Built Perfectly "In Tune"	76
The Effects of Temperature	77
The Pitch Standard under Extreme Temperatures	78
Oboes and Bassoons are Special	78
The "Coin Trick"	78
How to Use the Clarinet as the Pitch Standard	79
Recommended Tuning Routine	79
Stretched Octaves	82
Visual Tuning Versus Aural Tuning	82
Where to Listen	83
Teenage Brain Reaction Time	84
Sounding the Pitch Routine	84
Adopt the Focus Concept for Sonority	84

Drifting Sharp 84
Summary 85
Important Rehearsal Resources 85

CHAPTER 11: THE MONOLITHIC BAND SOUND 88
The Finlandia Year 88
The Egmont Overture Episode 89
Alterations to the Original Published Score for Festival Use 90

CHAPTER 12: PROPER ARTICULATION 92
Don't Say "Tut", Say "Da" 92
Brass Tongue Placement 92
Woodwind Tongue Placement 93

PART 3: TEACHING TECHNIQUES AND SUGGESTIONS

CHAPTER 13: ROTE VERSUS FUNDAMENTALS 96
Routines 98
Discipline 98
Teaching Aesthetics 99
Moral Values 99

CHAPTER 14: "I TAUGHT IT, BUT DID THEY REALLY LEARN IT?" 102

CHAPTER 15: WAYS TO DEVELOP A BETTER EAR 104
The Transformation 105
Hearing: The Most Important Skill 105
Ways to Acquire "Band Director Ears" 106
Solving the Problem of Poor Acoustics 110
Hearing Musically is a Constant Challenge 110

CHAPTER 16: THE CRITICAL CONFIDANT 112
The Nature of the Job 112
The Critical Confidant 112
Perspective 113
If at First You Don't Succeed 114

CHAPTER 17: HOST A GUEST CONDUCTOR 117

CHAPTER 18: THE GIANT METRONOME 121

CHAPTER 19: THE MEMORIZE & LOOK-UP TECHNIQUE FOR OUTSTANDING PERFORMANCE 124
The Technique 125
Look Up For Entrances 126

PART 4: MUSIC & MUSIC PREPARATION

CHAPTER 20: METHOD BOOKS 129
- How to Use Beginning Method Books 129
- What to Do When the Method Book Gets Dull 129
- More Flexible Conductor Method Book Manuals 130
- Beyond the Method Books 130
- A System of Counting 131
- Sonority Training 131
- Embouchure Training 132
- Establishing Practice Habits 132

CHAPTER 21: MARKING MUSIC 133
- Markings to Consider 133
- *NOBLE MEN* - by Henry Fillmore 134

CHAPTER 22: FOLIO MANAGEMENT 135
- Miscellaneous Parts 135
- Labeling Folios 135
- Two Sets of Folios 135
- Performance Folios 136
- Catalog Each Sheet of Music 136
- The Jazz Band "Book" 136
- Sheet Music 137

CHAPTER 23: PREPARATION AND PERFORMANCE OF MARCHES 139
- The Medium 140
- Grading 140
- Compositional Structure 141
- Styling of Standard Marches for Concert Performance 142
- Some Styling Ideas by Section 144
- Ideas on Rehearsing Standard Marches 145
- Recommended CD Recordings 147
- Other References 148

PART 5: FESTIVAL PREPARATION IDEAS

CHAPTER 24: FESTIVALS AND CONTESTS 151
- The Road to a Superior at State Festival: A Summary 152
- One of the Biggest Mistakes 153
- The Fundamentals 154
- Music Selection 154
- The Sound 156

    RECOMMENDED READING 157

CHAPTER 25: COUNTDOWN TO A SUPERIOR 159
    FOR SOLO AND ENSEMBLE FESTIVAL 159
    PREPARATION FOR SOLO AND ENSEMBLE FESTIVAL 159
    THE COUNTDOWN 160

CHAPTER 26: THE "DOCTOR'S OFFICE" ROUTINE FOR COACHING SOLOS AND ENSEMBLES 166
    HERE IS HOW IT WORKS 166
    MOTIVATION 168
    ACCOMPANISTS 168
    SCHEDULING 169
    PERFORMING 169

PART 6: SECRETS FOR SUCCESS IN THE BANDROOM

CHAPTER 27: ENSEMBLE SEATING BY CHALLENGING 172
    THE CHALLENGE CONTRACT AS A TOOL FOR ESTABLISHING SEATING 172
    TWO DANGERS 172
    RULES FOR CHALLENGING 173

CHAPTER 28: A COLLECTION OF TIPS FOR SUCCESS 176
    SUCCESS IN STARTING FRENCH HORN PLAYERS 176
    HERE ARE SOME ADVANTAGES 176
    A TOOL TO PULL STUCK SWABS 180
    THE MYSTERY OF THE SQUEAKING CLARINETS PART 2 181
    LAMINATE FAVORITE SHEET MUSIC 181
    REQUIRING PRACTICE SCHEDULES 181
    PLAYING TESTS 182
    THE "DO IT AGAIN" RULE 182
    MARK PARTS BEFOREHAND 183
    A VISUAL WAY TO TEACH DYNAMICS 183
    MUTES CHANGE PITCH 185
    "TUT" IS BAD 186
    EXECUTING A BALANCED CRESCENDO AND DIMINUENDO 186

CHAPTER 29: MEDICAL TREATMENT PERMISSION 189

CHAPTER 30: PERSONAL PHILOSOPHY 190
    THE DANGER OF HAVING VIEWS 190
    SUPPORT ONE ANOTHER AND OUR PROFESSION 190
    DON'T MAKE RASH DECISIONS 191
    FESTIVAL IDEAS 191

    Marching Band 192

CHAPTER 31: MORE TIPS ON BECOMING A BETTER BAND DIRECTOR............194
    Get Out of Town 194
    The Thing To Do.. 194
    Fundamentals 195
    The Listening Festival Idea... 195
    Band Literature Yesterday and Today... 196
    The "Thing To Do" or "Not The Thing To Do" 197

PART 7: RETROSPECTIVE

CHAPTER 32: MY RECOLLECTIONS OF HENRY FILLMORE 200
    A Few Stories about Henry Before I Knew Him... 200
    When I Knew Him 201
    The University of Miami Band Camps 202
    Miami Band Tours 203

BIBLIOGRAPHY 205

BIOGRAPHIES 210

Preface to the Second Edition by Catherine McNamara

William Clayton Miller is my Uncle and the author of a wonderful book, *Band Director's Secrets for Success*. It was a difficult decision to create an updated issue of my uncle's book and I approached this project with great apprehension. Part of me wanted to keep "The Book" (as we all called it) a sacred text. Then, one day, I had an epiphany that made me realize how important it is to bring this updated edition to the band world.

My university studies and subsequent career focused on elementary curriculum design and visual arts instruction; however, I have had the privilege of playing in a variety of bands throughout my adult life. I have often wondered why many directors stop repeatedly during rehearsals to teach notes or to work on intonation. Many times I have asked myself: "Wouldn't it be easier if the band directors would simply teach the players how to play in tune and how to listen correctly rather than stopping every few measures to tune notes?"

One day, while sitting patiently during one such stop, the answer hit me like a ton of bricks. The band directors work this way because they were **never taught** how to teach the group these simple techniques! Being a student in Uncle Bill's band had completely spoiled me. This became a frequent subject of conversation between myself and Uncle Bill's protégé and my good friend, Dr. N. Alan Clark. We knew these directors to be dedicated and intelligent professionals who care deeply about producing quality music, but these basic skills are not part of the music curriculum in many universities. It was at that moment I realized I had an obligation to try to make Uncle Bill's teachings available to as many band directors as possible. Over the course of his career, Uncle Bill developed the ability to teach these seemingly ineffable concepts. In his book, Uncle Bill clearly describes how any band director willing to apply these simple techniques can build a "monster band" program.

The depth of knowledge of both musicianship and application of educational philosophies have been meticulously expanded and incorporated into this new volume by Dr. Clark. My experience as an educator, in developing award winning, integrated curricula, and former student of Uncle Bill's band allows me a special appreciation for the solid ideas presented here. This new version of

"The Book" breathes new life into the wonderful concepts Uncle Bill developed over his long teaching career.

Through the years one of my favorite things has been when one of Uncle Bill's former students tells me what being in his band meant to them. The common element is always this: "We accomplished so much that normal high school musicians just can't do. He created a learning environment that made it easier to be a high achiever than it was to be lazy and underachieve. That one lesson is what has made me a better (doctor, lawyer, mother, father…)" That was Uncle Bill's special gift and now it can be yours too. Go forth and make great bands!

Catherine McNamara

Preface to the Second Edition by N. Alan Clark

This book is a labor of love. Bill loved it and I love it. The enthusiasm it has generated since it was first published in 1997 indicates that others have learned to love it as well. Like any human endeavor this book, *"The Book"* as Bill called it, is not without its blemishes. This edition attempts to smooth out a few minor wrinkles and add supportive references where appropriate. I also added a few chapters compiled from Bill's notes and our conversations. The original edition was a treasure trove of concepts and techniques amassed over Bill's long and superb career as a teacher, clinician, and judge. None of that has been altered or removed.

The book is organized with the topics Bill considered most important up front; beginning with Idealism and Mentorship and progressing through Expectation Level and Bandsman Attitude and Motivation, before arriving at the important technique-specific chapters such as Proper Embouchure Focus, Buzzing, Dwelling, and Projection. The final two chapters were constructed from Bill's notes for presentations he gave at Florida Bandmasters Association summer conventions.

It is my sincere hope that mentors and students alike will use this edition, like the first, to continue the work for which it was originally intended – to promote and enhance teaching and learning in school bands across America.

Major N. Alan Clark, Ph.D., USAF (ret.)

Preface to the First Edition by William Clayton Miller

[This is Mr. Miller's original Preface from 1997]

This book is a collection of topics on teaching school band. For many years I was bothered by the lack of dialog among band director colleagues on many important subjects. Many concepts were seldom discussed, yet they were the very essence of what it takes to develop a fine sounding ensemble. This book is the result of an effort to share some helpful pedagogic "tools" that have proven to be invaluable.

It's been my good fortune to have had opportunities to learn from some of the most outstanding people in the band field. I feel lucky that certain events allowed me to learn important concepts about teaching band. After the formal education, the most important factor that determines the quality of our work is what we learn from each other. This profession demands knowledge so broad, varied, and complex that it's not likely one individual is expert enough to "go it alone", so we must seek help from colleagues. Early in my career I began to realize certain things about teaching band that were vitally important to the success of the program, yet were generally unknown. In this book it's my intention to share some of the most important concepts in teaching band.

Over the years I have observed that much of what is necessary for success is not generally known. It's almost as if there are well-guarded "secrets" that only certain directors know and never tell anyone. Directors entering the field for the first time look forward to a rewarding career of building and maintaining a high quality band program. Although our music schools have never before done a better job preparing new music teachers, there are still important aspects that are sometimes overlooked. Hopefully in these pages some of the vital elements that have been illusive will be made clearer and be of significant benefit to the reader.

I experienced building two school bands from humble beginnings to fully developed programs. The first was in a small town and ranged from teaching beginners in the sixth grade through senior high band. This started as a "one man operation" with 40 band members in the entire program. In the span of twelve years the program grew to two directors working with over 300 students. Later I built a program in a large high school where it was possible to develop many outstanding students and to explore the best in band literature.

I owe much of my success to my active participation in professional organizations. Membership in the Florida Bandmaster's Association has been valuable. I served two terms as a District Chairman in that organization and I continue to serve as adjudicator. The resulting contact with colleagues through the Florida Bandmasters Association (FBA) has played a vital role in developing a successful career. Also valuable has been membership in the Florida Music Educators Association (FMEA) which is directly linked to the Music Educators National Conference (MENC). The National Band Association (NBA) and American School Band Directors Association (ASBDA) have been valuable links to band activities on the national scene.

I've found there are a few outstanding personalities who, while very effective practitioners at band directing, are not easily conversant about their work. It seems some experts have difficulty explaining what they do and why they do it. Still, others are able to discuss their work eloquently. There is much to be learned from either type. It sometimes takes close observation, analysis, and careful listening to discover what's going on. Most master band directors are easily approached and are most anxious to share their knowledge. It's important not to be reticent about asking about the many aspects of this work.

At any age we must be constantly inquisitive and keep learning.

It's good practice to attend clinic presentations from the masters, constantly picking up on everything the experts have to offer. Two of the most significant clinic presentation events of my career are discussed in this book. Nilo Hovey went about the country some years ago with a presentation I found most valuable. The idea is to tune the clarinet section to itself, then tune the rest of the band to the clarinets. (The details of this are in chapter nine.) Another valuable offering came from Claude Gordon. He described a technique where brass players can quickly build stamina. I gave this technique the name "squeeze play." (See chapter four.)

In earlier years the Florida Bandmasters Association devoted most of the meeting time to details about the administration of the district and state evaluation festivals. From the beginning of my career I was an advocate of using the association meetings to also offer "how to do it" clinics; forums where band directors could share their expertise. As time has passed, more attention has been given to meeting the broader needs of the members through information and "how to do it" clinics.

Experiences from judging band festivals have offered many opportunities to see and hear the developmental patterns of many student players and to observe what other band directors are doing.

Other opportunities to observe and work with many students from diverse backgrounds came from the twenty years I taught summer band camps. The wonderful five-week camp at the University of Miami, Coral Gables, Florida was run by Fred McCall, Director of Bands at the University. Students came from all over and many varied musical and cultural backgrounds. Eventually the enrollment grew to over five hundred campers. Camp offerings included five concert bands, full orchestra, two jazz bands, and theory classes at all levels, private lessons from outstanding teachers, and many organized musical and entertainment events. The staff was made up of mostly public school band directors. Only university faculty who worked well with school age students was hired. There were several leaders in the band field teaching at the camp. A good friend and colleague was Otto Kraushaar, one of the most outstanding band directors in the history of the band movement. Otto had been a bassoonist in the Sousa Band and he had good advice about many aspects of the band profession. Once he told me, "You start getting state festival "superiors" from the first day the student blows the instrument, not from just working hard a few months before the festival." He was referring to the importance of laying down a strong foundation in the fundamentals right from the very first moments the student touches the instrument.

One outstanding feature of the University of Miami camp was that no director conducted just one ensemble all of the time. All directors conducted and taught all levels. Besides offering the students experiences with many directors, it also gave the directors opportunities to work with many students and to observe and share knowledge with colleagues. When McCall retired from the University of Miami, the camp moved to Webber College in Lake Wales, Florida. The staff was virtually the same in both places.

Working the camps offered a unique opportunity to observe over a period of several years how students from many programs were developing on their instruments. This opportunity proved to be most significant. For me it all added up to some twenty years of being on the staff of an outstanding five-week long summer band camp. From the varied experiences of working with so many student players from many backgrounds I came to realize the significance and pervasiveness of a serious problem that exists in school bands and in developing student player...pinched embouchures. I have come to realize the true nature of this problem goes undetected by most students and teachers. This is such an elusive problem that many teachers fail to realize it as a fundamental error in student player development. Discussion of this problem will receive much attention in this book.

On five separate occasions I was invited to give clinic presentations for the Florida Bandmasters Association at the annual Florida Music Educators Association All - State Clinics. For each of these sessions I decided to reproduce and distribute the entire clinic text in booklet format to allow the attendees to take a reference home with them. Many times clinicians choose not to prepare or distribute printed materials for their presentations. I believe that this is an unfortunate oversight and I was determined not to fall into the same trap. I paid for the printing out of my own pocket, but what seemed at the time to be a little extravagant turned out to be well worth the effort. Many band directors who missed the clinics have asked for copies of the booklets and their popularity has motivated me to expand the topics and present them under one cover.

A few years ago I sent the first three booklets to the late John Paynter. While attending the Midwest clinic the following year I met him in the hallway and he quoted to me from one of the articles. I was surprised to learn that he frequently used the first three and I told him that another had been completed. He asked for a copy and one week after receiving it he called and asked if he could use all four in his graduate methods class! I immediately called my friend of many years Mr. Frank Wickes, the Director of Bands at Louisiana State

University, and he urged me to begin the project that ultimately produced this book.

Captain Norman Alan Clark, Commander and Conductor of the Command Band of the Air Force Reserve, Robins AFB, Georgia, has been involved with this book since first writing. His help was invaluable in proof reading and editing. Several topics were included and discussed because of his help with this project including contributions in the area of woodwind pedagogy. I owe him my appreciation for his interest, work, and encouragement during the development of this project.

Lieutenant Jeff Warner, Deputy Commander of the Command Band of the Air Force Reserve, Robins AFB, Georgia, offered several helpful suggestions as the book developed. Prior to entering the Air Force, Jeff was the Band and Orchestra Director at the Cypress Lakes School of the Arts in Ft. Myers, Florida where he very successfully applied many of the techniques presented here.

Chief Master Sergeant Dave Ballengee, who served as both Director of Tours and International Affairs, and as Guest Artist Producer for The United States Air Force Band, provided many invaluable philosophical insights and contributed much to the chapter on the philosophy of "Expectation Level."

• • •

PART 1:

PHILOSOPHICAL UNDERPINNINGS

Chapter 1: Ideals and Mentorship

"Mentoring is a brain to pick, an ear to listen, and a push in the right direction."

--John C. Crosby

Every director is aware of that gray area between what one must do to meet the minimum requirements of the job, and what must be done to make the program outstanding in quality and offering. This is the challenge in any line of work. The truth is, the young band director is aware of this factor and, in some way, inwardly decides where the boundaries are; how far will they walk that extra mile to offer more than the minimum that is required.

Essentially, what are the young director's "ideals?" Almost everyone entering a profession is young and energetic and is initially idealistic; out to show the world what a terrific job they are going to do. Most new band directors believe they are going to do an outstanding job and develop a superior school musical organization. However, many times these young directors seem to abandon their ideals very quickly. Within a short time they no longer put forth the effort it takes to get the job done. Why? What are the factors that defeat the initially idealistic new teacher? What causes so many to either quit, or fall into mediocrity for the rest of their teaching career?

In many of these cases new teachers are unable to land a job that offers hope for outstanding results. Many can only find a job in situations that are so limited that no teacher, no matter how experienced and qualified, could make anything of it other than teach at the most basic level - yielding results far below the norm. Two years of discouragement and failure seem to be about the limit most new teachers can take. Then, as if a giant steel door closes before them, the once promising new member of the music teaching force withdraws into a shell of discouraged complacency.

What a terrible indictment; yet, all too often, this is exactly what happens. Let's examine this unfortunate reversal and look for a possible solution. Inwardly, psychologically what these young teachers experience in frustration and dejection may be summarized like this: "I did the best I could do. With all my effort and ability I still fell short; if that isn't good enough, to hell with it!"

[Bill never finished this chapter. We talked about it many times and it was intended to be included in the second iteration of "The Book." The remainder of this chapter is based on our many discussions of a powerful solution – mentorship – and derives from an article I wrote for the *NBA Journal* (Clark, 2008).]

Rekindling the Culture of Mentorship

N. Alan Clark

When I started teaching in 1976, I was very, very fortunate – only I didn't know it then. I was mentored, almost weekly and very thoroughly, by two Florida Bandmasters Association Hall of Fame directors -- William C. "Bill" Miller and Tom Bishop. One or the other, and sometimes both, of these outstanding educators would visit my junior high band rehearsals at least once every week or two and neither of them had any problem telling me "what you need to do now is…" What invaluable instruction and what incredible good fortune for me. Many of my career successes are due to the foundation laid by these two unselfish men. Many of my rehearsal techniques, administrative habits, and recruiting ideas originated with them in those early years.

Bill was the director of bands at Lakeland (FL) High School and Tom was our Polk County Supervisor of Music. Both saw my success as very important to the overall success of the Lakeland band as well as the band movement in Polk County and I certainly wasn't the only one they helped. I never fell on my face because they didn't allow it to happen. They saw to it that I didn't step on any parental or administrative land mines and that I programmed the right music and rehearsed the right things. They taught me how to reinforce excellent tonal concepts using the stereo system in my band room, how to record and objectively review my rehearsals, and how to teach counting using what we called the Eastman counting system. They taught me the value of sight-reading every rehearsal and how to "routine" the band for maximum rehearsal effectiveness. They taught me how to prepare a budget and how to work with the band parent organization, coaches, and administration. Neither Tom nor Bill ever asked for anything in return. Their support for me was without ego and noble in that it was only intended to promote the ideal of bettering the band community. That ideal was a driving force throughout both of their lives.

During the 1970s many marching band directors began to emulate drum corps…much good came from this. I am a big fan of Drum Corps International (DCI), having served as a marching instructor with Suncoast Sound during the mid-1980s. I learned a great deal from my time in DCI and highly recommend it to young directors (those who can actually sleep on gym floors.) Following the lead of DCI, marching band show designers began to design their shows to face the audience throughout the performance thereby enhancing the connection between the performers and the people. Designers began to coordinate the band and its auxiliary components in such a way as to promote a central theme; this was a radical break from traditional picture shows and squad-based and step-two designs. The DCI influence radically advanced the pedagogy of school percussion playing and instruction and also created a much more sophisticated colorguard culture. Many band directors began to focus more on the fundamentals of brass, percussion, and colorguard performance – all of these changes improved marching band performance.

One not-so-good thing that came out of this decade was a misapplication by some band directors of the competitive culture. By "misapplication" I mean a focus on secrecy and withholding of ideas, concepts, and techniques for the sake of winning. This culture of secrecy encouraged some directors to keep to themselves and their programs and not to reach out to younger directors in their local areas. Interestingly, I recall many instances during my years in DCI of the sharing of ideas and even staff members between corps – maybe more than the members realized at the time! I am very encouraged to see that the pendulum seems to be swinging back towards a mentoring culture. Recent efforts encouraging mentorship by such organizations as the Midwest Clinic, NBA, and NAfME certainly have not gone unnoticed or unappreciated.

The transition from college study to school teaching is a complicated process. Even the best college music education programs cannot compress every experience a young teacher needs into an undergraduate curriculum. There isn't enough time. Some degree of on-the-job training is inevitable. There are many administrative, organizational, public relations, management, and teaching techniques that aspiring band directors must master in order to be successful. Some of these techniques are learned in the normal course of on-the-job training, but many of the most important ones aren't. Knowledge of these important "secrets" must be offered by capable and dedicated mentors and must be readily accepted by open minded and dedicated novice directors. The future of our profession depends on this!

When we were beginning teachers, most of us appreciated the patient, honest mentoring that we received from those who preceded us. Young teachers today are no different and most will appreciate any advice or encouragement. Many of us who have been at it a while, can do much to grow and strengthen our bands by patiently mentoring and encouraging our young band directors. But we also have to ask ourselves one important question. Do we still love the profession enough to be a positive influence on the next generation? Successful young directors positively impact every facet of bands in America from elementary school to the pros and including the music industry; not to mention the focus of the whole process – the students. Let's throw some logs on the fire and do what we can to help them be successful.

So, how do we actually do this mentorship thing? First, take the time and make an effort to develop a relationship. Strive to be a good listener and allow the young teacher to direct the conversation. Let their needs and concerns influence your strategy. Here are a few suggestions of areas that might benefit from your attention. There are others. Feel free to add to and modify this list for your own situation.

Recruiting and Building a Strong Beginning Band Program

1. Developing positive relationships with music teachers and administrators in feeder schools

2. Recruiting performances at feeder schools

3. Targeting future band students

4. The rental program meeting

5. The rental/purchase question

6. Educating the music store – what you expect in quality, mouthpieces, etc.

7. How to convince students to play needed instruments

8. How to select and use method books.

9. Add your own modifications to this list

Rehearsals

1. Long-range rehearsal planning based on a long-range performance calendar planning

2. Rehearsal discipline

3. Motivation

4. How to "hear" what's really going on

5. Selection of repertoire for strengths of ensemble

6. Score study – every chord, or the big picture?

7. Constructive critique of rehearsal techniques

8. How to structure a successful rehearsal

9. Tone production fundamentals for all winds

10. How to tune the ensemble and how to teach the students to listen

11. How to pace the rehearsal

12. Unique characteristics and problems of the instruments

13. Suggested repertoire and methods

14. Good quality solo and ensemble repertoire

Administration of the Band and the Band Booster Organization

1. How to interact with the administration (and their egos)
2. Public relations with the community and administration
3. How to support (and benefit from) school athletics
4. How to organize the booster organization
5. How to guide the band booster organization
6. The band budget
7. Fundraising in the local area

• • •

Chapter 2: Expectation Level

"Don't lower your expectations to meet your performance. Raise your performance to meet your expectations."

--Roger Marston

One of the most important and least understood concepts affecting band performance is the concept of "expectation level." High expectations may, in fact, be considered a secret weapon. In psychology this concept is known as the Pygmalion Effect...the idea that an individual or a group will achieve what they are expected to achieve. J. Sterling Livingston discusses the Pygmalion Effect in more detail in the September 1969 issue of the *Harvard Business Review* (Livingston, 1969). This concept has also been referred to as a self-fulfilling prophecy.

It is critical that the leader communicate frequently, and in a positive way, that he expects the group to perform exceedingly well. The director who constantly complains and derides his band will get the product he programmed his students to deliver...failure. Likewise, the director that openly expects excellence from his students will program his group to produce superior results. Accept only the best that your students are capable of providing every time. Let them know what you expect and that you know that they will succeed.

Positive reinforcement is far superior to negative reinforcement. Many of us were trained in an environment that was based on some degree of negative reinforcement, sometimes to the extreme. Yelling at students, belittling them, even throwing things was not only tolerated, it was often admired! Being "mean" was considered the same as being "demanding" and meanness was equated with having high standards. Tyrants were looked upon as great leaders who were never to be questioned or challenged! Actually quite the opposite is true. Remember that the Pygmalion Effect works in both directions. Too much negative feedback can have the effect of training students to expect failure. Creating an environment that "drives out fear from the workplace'" allows musicians to be more relaxed and therefore to play much better than when they feel threatened. This is one of the key points presented by W. Edwards Deming, the great Total Quality Management guru, in his fascinating book Out of the Crisis (1986).

Music is a subjective and sensitive art form. People on the defensive will not relax enough to access their deeper, subjective feelings. They will always play it safe and never be as expressive as they could be in a less threatening environment. High standards are **very** important, critical to a superior band program, and are achieved through having both a high expectation level and using positive reinforcement. Let your students know how proud you are of them, frequently! They will respond.

Provide your students with a never-ending series of positive role models (guest conductors, guest artists, videotaped performances of outstanding groups or individuals, trips to attend concerts by great performers, recordings, [YouTube], etc.) Remember also that there are three basic levels of discipline: Imposed discipline which is imposed on the individual from the outside, group discipline which grows out of peer pressure from the group, and self-discipline which is the self-imposed highest level of discipline. Strive to develop an environment that will encourage the growth of self-discipline.

I had great success building strong band programs by expecting every bandsman to do a great job. I fully expected the students to deserve "A's" and therefore they did. Doesn't the grade of "C" mean "average"? Would you like to listen to a band with many of the bandsmen playing at an "average" level?

Actually, to have a fine band, all players must be "A" level players. In a strong, successful band, performing at even a "B" level is a serious liability. For band students, a "B" is actually a low grade. I found that just expecting everyone to work at an "A" level was all it took to get everyone doing their best.

Understand and accept the fact that you are going to have to remind your students over and over again. They are human. They won't remember much of what you tell them from day to day. Don't get impatient; get in the habit of patiently reminding them of sonority, of balance, intonation, and precision (BIP), and of what it takes to be good band members. They want to do well...expect them to. Patience and persistence will prove much more effective than cajoling and chastising, every time. The group's capability and the bottom line level of all of your performances will never exceed your expectation level and/or your ability to provide the "vision" of where they can and should be.

Rehearsals: We have been trained to rehearse, rehearse, and rehearse, to keep doing it until we "get it right." However, the subliminal message that this approach sends may not be the message we really intend. For example, imagine having 20 rehearsals to prepare a program. The students inevitably subconsciously adopt the mind-set of taking the entire 20 rehearsals to get ready. The product probably won't improve noticeably until 17 or 18 of the rehearsals are used up. Scheduling numerous lengthy rehearsals actually suggests to students that they can't prepare music like the "Pros" do, so why should they try?

Why not try another approach? Try telling the group that you only have a few (three or four) rehearsals to prepare something and watch what happens. Tell them that you are amazed at how much they have improved during the year and that you feel that they are ready to start rehearsing in a more "professional" manner. Train them to expect to do it right the first time, and then press ahead. You might be surprised at the results!

Professional studio musicians don't become "first-take" quality players because producers schedule multiple rehearsals and three or four recording sessions for one recording! The understanding up-front is that the musicians must produce the first time, so they do! Remember the great college football coaches? Bear Bryant, Bobby Bowden, and Steve Spurrier expected the best from their players year after year and they got it regardless of the player's innate talent. If you go out there and expect the best, you'll get it!

• • •

Chapter 3: Bandsman Attitude and Motivation

"It's your attitude, not your aptitude that determines your altitude."

--Zig Ziglar

Another very significant factor that determines the success of a band is the attitude of the band members. Below are a few important sources and concepts that will help the reader establish and maintain positive attitudes throughout the band program.

The Band Director's Brain Bank

Jack Mercer in his book *The Band Director's Brain Bank* (1970) describes a study he did which searched for characteristics that are shared by successful band directors. Mercer tried to find correlations: Did successful directors come from large or a small high school bands? Did they come from good or bad quality high school or college bands? Were they outstanding or average musicians? Were they well organized or not? Nothing in his results correlated except one thing: With every successful band director Mercer found "he was well liked and respected." This book is available through *The Instrumentalist* magazine. Mercer discusses several other important issues concerning bands. It is a very worthwhile read.

The Pyramid of Success

An excellent plan for building good attitudes in band members can be found in a book about coaching basketball. Chapter 12 of this book, *They Call Me Coach* (1988) by John Wooden, former basketball coach at UCLA, gives a detailed explanation of Coach Wooden's famous "Pyramid of Success." When you study coach Wooden's pyramid, substitute the band for the basketball team and consider how to apply the techniques to band "team" members. You will be amazed at the numerous similarities! Another great contribution in this book is Coach Wooden and his definition of success:

Coach Wooden's Definition of Success:

The peace of mind which is a direct result of the self-satisfaction of knowing you did your best to become the best you are capable of becoming.

This philosophy is exactly what we should teach students when preparing to enter a festival or contest of any kind!

The Definition of a Winner:

A winner is a person who did the best he could, regardless of any rating or final reward. Only the individual knows within him/herself if he/she is a winner.

Ratings, such as "superior", "excellent", etc. indicate the quality of a performance as judged by others. They do not reveal the true winner. A student with above average talent who easily wins a "superior" rating by only half trying isn't necessarily a winner. But, the student with average ability who works hard and does his or her very best, whatever the final rating, is a winner.

A Winning Teaching Philosophy

I believe that teaching from a morality-based point of view is the most successful way to build a strong band program. I have learned that the most successful directors are the ones who get through to their students using this approach. They teach from the standpoint of positive motivation. They mold strong individual bandsmen who are intensely loyal to the band and the director. It's this moral conscience, constantly at work in each bandsman that underpins most fine band programs. A band must, of course, have rules for playing, participation, and achievement. But these rules must not be the ends in themselves; rather they must be in the background. Yes, there needs to be a band handbook that states all the requirements, rules, and consequences, but these must be looked upon only as the operating instructions for the band, not as the ultimate goals. For example, playing a piece of music with all the right notes, rhythms, and interpretations should be taught as a moral obligation each bandsman has to the band. Conversely, not being able to play the part is equivalent to letting down all of the other members.

In my early teaching years I tried other methods. I found that requiring students to turn in practice schedules, using a demerit system, and severe grading systems were all counterproductive. When I switched to the approach described above, the band program greatly improved. My work became more effective, and I became a more successful band director. The most successful directors are the ones who teach their bandsmen to want to make the band as good as possible. There are usually very few rules, everyone is on time for all rehearsals and performances, very few members are absent from rehearsals and performances (no one ever "just doesn't show up"), all the bandsmen work hard, and all are highly motivated. It would be unthinkable for any member to "let the band down." This morality based philosophy takes hard work to instill, but it provides a very powerful and successful foundation for a band program.

Music educators are well aware of the magnetic power of the fine arts, the driving force that seems to be associated with teaching aesthetic values. It's probably one of the main reasons we ourselves joined the profession. There are few teachers in our schools today with the potential power of combining the two forces of moral virtues and aesthetics. The band director has that power!

• • •

PART 2:
TONE, TUNING AND ARTICULATION

Chapter 4: Proper Embouchure Focus

"That's been one of my mantras – focus and simplicity. Simple can be harder than complex: You have to work hard to get your thinking clean to make it simple. But it's worth it in the end because once you get there, you can move mountains."

--Steve Jobs

What is about to be presented here is what I consider to be the single most important concept necessary for the development of superior wind instrumentalists. This one factor over all others makes the biggest difference in the development of a superior band sound. And it is usually what determines the difference between students being rated "superior" and those being rated "excellent" for any type of festival entry (soloist, jazz band, small ensemble, or full concert band).

Unfortunately, many band performances suffer due to poor intonation and tone quality. Although the technical aspects of these performances (correct notes, correct rhythms, precision, etc.) are often properly executed, these ensembles still sound bad. All too often well-disciplined, well-equipped bands enthusiastically performing top quality literature will fall short because their basic sound is mediocre. Much work in preparation of the other musical elements may be evident. The players' technical mastery may be outstanding, yet when nagging intonation and tone problems persist the resulting musical effect is poor. Certainly teaching band students the names of the notes, scales, rhythm patterns, and how to read printed music is vitally important. Most directors do a good job of teaching these elements. However, the fundamental element of good sonority must be considered first. Let me say it again- in order to be successful, bands must perform with a mature tone quality and excellent intonation. The most thorough and excellent fundamental instruction coupled with superior student technique will result in compromised results if this one aspect of playing -- fine sonority -- is not successfully taught and mastered by all players.

Can every singly wind player in an ensemble be taught to sound good? Yes they can! Even inexperienced players can play with good tone quality and acceptable intonation if they learn to play with proper embouchure focus. Consider the best high school bands you have ever heard. It is probably safe to say that not all of the members of these groups are outstanding players. But even with a mixture of experienced and inexperienced performers these bands sound good because the directors have successfully taught every member to play with a good sound.

As I said before, wind players, regardless of level, from beginning students to the most mature, can be taught to achieve an excellent sound. This is not some super-secret advanced level of band development that is obtained only after years of training. It is possible for a sixth or seventh grade beginning band to perform with very good intonation and tone. Not only is it possible, it should be the number one goal!

Sonority

Sonority may be thought of as a combination of a mature characteristic tone, good intonation, and good balance.

Mature Tone

Excellent sonority is achieved only when all players produce a mature characteristic tone on their instruments. Good intonation is impossible with improper tone production. A properly produced, professional sounding tone will get the players very close to pitch center. Then they only need to make very slight, not large, adjustments to achieve good intonation.

Good Intonation

In order to play in tune, wind instrumentalists must develop playing stamina. Stamina is simply the ability to play with and control a correctly focused embouchure. Breath control is also important. Members must be taught to 'hear' musically. They need to be taught who to listen to, where to listen, and how to adjust pitches in order to obtain good intonation. It initially takes time to teach these concepts, but they are critical! Simply saying, "listen down to the tubas" is not the answer. Sometimes band members cannot hear the tubas. Sometimes the tubas aren't playing. The woodwinds often sit in front of the trumpets or trombones. In these situations can they really hear the tubas? Listening to those nearby, to those with the same melody or counter melody, or those with the same chord tone often makes much more practical sense – and is also one of the many things professional musicians do, in every situation. Learning to actively listen to everything is a much better approach than simply listening to the tubas.

Good Balance

The band must have good balance so all players can hear each other across the ensemble. Balance largely depends on instrumentation. If the instrumentation is not balanced it may be necessary for the director to switch players to other instruments in order to achieve proper instrumental balance.

Vocabulary

This brief list of terms is intended to aid in the identification and labeling of certain elements affecting wind instrument tone production.

> Stamina: The physical strength and conditioning necessary to produce, control, and sustain a characteristic tone on a wind instrument

> Poise: The ability to maintain, control, and sustain proper embouchure shape

Focus: The ability to poise the embouchure attained by developing adequate stamina

Sonority: The combination of:

1. Good balance that allows all performers to hear one another

2. All performers possessing a characteristic tone

3. All performers possessing the ability to adjust pitch and play in tune

Simply put, sonority is the product of tone, intonation, and balance.

The Embouchure Focus

Over the years I have observed that **most** student brass players initially play with a pinched embouchure. I have also observed that student woodwind players tend to use too much bite, particularly saxophonists. The students don't realize this, and many teachers are unaware of what the problem is and therefore fail to correct it.

The incorrect, pinched embouchure is the single most pervasive bad habit and is responsible for many, if not most, playing problems.

When students have poor endurance, limited range, poor response, and sharp upper registers it is almost always due to embouchure pinching or biting.

Players Must Be Taught

1. How to focus the embouchure correctly

2. How to develop the embouchure (physically)

3. What to listen for so they know where to adjust their embouchure

> Achieving fine sonority by each player and collectively by the entire ensemble is fundamental to developing a fine sounding band.

Teaching sonority is fundamental. This aspect of training wind players should be the top priority because, if good sonority is not achieved, all other aspects of playing are ruined. Once understood, good sonority is no more difficult to teach than any other musical element. Remember, for the individual player to achieve good sonority he/she must have the ability to correctly focus the embouchure. The player must also know how to hear the rest of the ensemble so pitches can be matched while playing with a fine characteristic tone that is balanced and blended with the rest of the ensemble.

Of course, as I said before, all other aspects of musicianship must also be thoroughly taught. Students must know the technical skills of music: the names of notes, scales, rhythm patterns, and music reading. I have observed over the years that almost all band directors do well at teaching what's in the printed score. Even bands that receive low ratings at festival play the right notes, rhythms, and dynamics. It's what's not in the printed music that determines the quality of the performance.

Training Ensembles for Fine Sonority

It takes time to achieve the desired results. Attention must be given to building excellent sonority during every rehearsal. Devoting a few minutes of each rehearsal will produce significantly better sonority in two to three months. Successful musical growth has a positive influence on improving the general attitude of each player; and more dedication and devotion to the group results when the group sounds good. Over time, the satisfaction from consistent "superior" evaluations becomes a powerful influence on perpetuating consistent high standards and good fundamental habits. When the director is dedicated to consistently addressing and improving the group's sonority, individual responsibility for playing with superior tone quality becomes part of the group's culture.

Specifics Concerning Proper Embouchure Focus

For a wind player, achieving good intonation rests primarily on four main factors:

1. Players must tune their instruments correctly in order to have enough latitude for their embouchures to be able to compensate for certain notes that are not exactly in tune.

2. Players must be able to lip bad notes in tune. Keep in mind that on wind instruments, pitches are more easily lipped down than up. As I mentioned earlier, most student players make the mistake of either pinching or biting and their embouchures usually lack the stamina to be able to control the embouchure focus. Also, students who pinch or bite usually tune their instruments flat. This prohibits them from having the latitude to bring the flat notes up and it makes their instruments more out of tune with themselves. Proper tuning allows players enough flexibility to be able to lip bad notes in tune, and this means tuning the

instrument high enough that all discrepancies can be lipped **down** in various degrees. **Lipping down is good, lipping up is bad**.

3. Players must have the physical stamina to be able to control their embouchures and adjust out of tune notes. Most players lack this stamina unless special attention has been given to this in their training.

4. The player must be able to hear the entire ensemble so he/she will know where to focus the pitch and play in tune with other players. Students must be constantly reminded to "listen" and they must be taught who to listen to.

I'm a trumpet player and this is what I think when I play: "When I tune up I don't adjust the tuning slide for what I initially learned as my "embouchure center." Instead I push in a little extra and lip everything down (except the flat notes on the horn which I play on center). Does this statement mean I play sharp? No, because remember, I think "lip everything down", which brings everything in tune. By lipping all pitches down, then I actually bring all notes in tune to the A = 440 Hz standard. If I adjust the slide to where I first learned the "center" of my embouchure, I cannot play the flat notes around the 5th partial up to pitch (top space E in the treble clef on trumpet). If I adjust the slide to what I initially learned as embouchure center, I would be restricted to the inherent intonation problems of the instrument and not be able to bend pitches down to where they are in tune. Of course, I have to be sure I can hear who I'm playing with at all times so I know where to center my pitch. In the end it is all a matter of what I consider the center of my embouchure. Again, I am thinking that I am tuning sharp and lipping down compared to what I **initially** learned as a young player.

When asked about this concept, professional players will say that they play in the center of their embouchures. But what professionals call centered, student players will probably think of as about 20% more relaxed than they normally play. So initially it will seem to student musicians as if they are lipping down. It's all a matter of what players first learn as embouchure center.

The bad habits of biting and pinching can persist indefinitely if not addressed. Pinched embouchures are actually undeveloped and consequently uncontrollable. It is important to know that when students who have been playing with pinched embouchures try using the new system for the first time, they probably won't be able to control their tones. It will take a few sessions of woodwind long tones and brass lip slur drills to build up the stamina needed to control the focus of the embouchure. Students must be taught to be conscientious about building and maintaining the correct embouchure. Once a program to develop the proper embouchure focus is begun, progress is swift. In just a few rehearsals the sonority of the ensemble will dramatically improve!

Either by luck or just figuring it out on their own, some players may stumble upon the correct embouchure from the beginning. Fantastic! However, most student players don't. When embouchures are left uncorrected and pinching continues, finesse and superior control are impossible. When students pinch they are unable to adjust and the inherent intonation discrepancies of the instrument take over. A trumpet player with a pinched embouchure will have the tuning slide out too far, usually about an inch. With a correctly focused embouchure the tuning slide will be out a little less than half an inch on a trumpet (less than an inch on a trombone). In fact, Adolph Herseth, the long-time principal trumpet of the Chicago Symphony, is rumored to have had the receiver tubes on his trumpet slightly shortened to allow him to push his tuning slide in even more!

When woodwind players pinch, they are actually playing with too much "bite." Excessive biting causes a thin tone, sharp intonation in the upper register, poor response in the low register, fatigue, and often results in a sore lip. Hard reeds are **not** the solution. The reed strength should match the mouthpiece facing. Open mouthpieces require softer reeds than more closed mouthpieces. Many, if not most, mouthpieces sold in America are medium tip openings (C and D designations) and certainly don't need #4 reeds! Hard reeds are not macho. Does it really make sense to grip something hard when you want it to vibrate? No, it doesn't.

Don Menza, the fabulous saxophonist and composer, has a video on YouTube that offers excellent insights into why players should not use excessive embouchure tension (Menza, 2010). Also, listening to professionals with great "classical" sounds is necessary to help young players develop a concept of how they are supposed to sound. An excerpt of Daniel Deffayet playing alto saxophone in a recording of Mussorgsky's *Pictures at an Exhibition* is as good as it gets (Deffayet, 2009)!

The solution is a "poised" and relaxed embouchure, not a firm or hard embouchure. Tone quality is greatly affected by the amount of bite, the position of the tongue, the type of mouthpiece being used, the strength of the reed (and how it fits the mouthpiece), and the concept of sound in the player's ear. Woodwind players must be made aware of all of these embouchure variables and encouraged to experiment with each one. They must learn how it feels to play with an embouchure (and oral cavity) that is properly formed but relaxed enough not to hinder the reed's vibration.

There are many problems that come directly from pinched embouchures. Endurance is a problem; the lip tires easily. Dynamic range is limited. Players cannot play very softly with control and the tone distorts at loud dynamic levels. Attacks are often fuzzy and low register response for woodwinds is very limited.

Remember, a trumpet player with a pinched embouchure will have the tuning slide out an inch or more. This student will be playing the 5th partial notes flat (E, Eb, D), while upper G, high C, and related notes will still be sharp. Woodwinds should use only enough pressure to flatten and form the embouchure. More pressure than that will only lead to problems with tone, response, tuning, and endurance. Remember also, if they use too much bite pressure their upper register will still be sharp even if they are pulled out quite a bit. When all wind players in a band are using the proper embouchure focus, the ensemble tone will be dark and rich.

Tongue Position

Brass – The role of tongue position in brass playing is much discussed and documented. Essentially, when brass players play higher tones they raise their tongues and when they play lower tones they lower their tongues relative to the hard and soft palates. In fact, some writers have referred to lip slurs as tongue slurs. I agree with the basics of this pedagogy. However, woodwinds are a different story entirely.

Woodwind – In the 1970s Raymond Wheeler published results of his research into clarinet tongue position, which indicated that clarinetists actually raised their tongues for lower notes, and lowered their tongues for higher notes. A video excerpt of one of his early movies may be found on YouTube and is a must view for all band directors (Wheeler, 2010). The renowned clarinet soloist Jose Franch-Ballester may be seen in a video demonstrating and discussing these same tongue position concepts (Franch-Ballester, 2012).

In both instances it is critical to teach students to be aware of their tongue position and to learn to use it in order to maximize both control and tone quality in all registers. Remember, one size does not fit all! Brass and woodwinds require different shaped oral cavities.

Correcting the Pinched Embouchure

To correct this embouchure-pinching problem, try teaching the concept of "lip down, tune up." Suggest a change in the focus of the embouchure to 20% looser, to poise the embouchure more open and relaxed. Remember, from their point of reference, the students think they have always been playing with a centered embouchure.

The Proper Embouchure Focus is a Panacea!

This is a very bold statement to make: Playing with the proper embouchure focus approach is almost a panacea, a cure-all, for most of the problems that confront wind instrument players. I believe that it is. This one aspect of playing, when mastered by all wind players, will help more than anything else in developing outstanding sonority, response, dynamic range...all of the parts of the puzzle that aren't on the printed page! A well-conditioned, correctly focused embouchure is easy to achieve once the correct effort is made toward that end.

Practicing certain routines that emphasize long tones for all players, and additional lip slurs for brass players is the best way to develop the correct focus. A director must have students working long tone and lip slur routines in daily practice and must spend a portion of each rehearsal on specialized drills designed to train the ensemble how to focus the embouchure. Initial response to instruction in this new way of playing will reveal those students who have been having trouble with intonation and tone; they are not able to execute this technique; their embouchures seem inflexible. They may thoroughly understand what they are to do and have a keen desire to comply, only to find they cannot seem to make the embouchure do as directed. They will not be able to 'dip' or 'bend' a pitch. Most brass players will not be able to lip slur at first. In fact, asking an individual to do a simple lip slur is a quick way to determine if he has the ability to focus pitches and poise the embouchure. Woodwind overtone exercises are an excellent tool to teach students how the bite, tongue, lips, and air stream all affect tone and response. Those who can lip slur (or play woodwind overtones) will be able to focus pitches; those who can't will not. The pinched, inflexible embouchure is a bad habit formed when too little attention is given to the necessary specialized instruction and drill. It can be fixed.

This concept can and should be taught to all wind players. It can be taught in a full band class setting or it can be taught by private teachers. All embouchures must be systematically conditioned to develop adequate stamina. (Remember that embouchure poise is directly related to stamina.) It does not take a long time for a player to master the correct focus and play with good sonority. Once the conditioning program is established, it takes only a few weeks for an entire band to build adequate stamina to master embouchure poise.

Even though the pinched embouchure syndrome is found in students at all stages of development, it can be corrected quickly once the student understands the problem and what to do about it. The embouchure focus and ability to poise the embouchure can be achieved with beginners. As I said earlier, it is entirely possible for a first year band to achieve very fine sonority.

Stamina Development for the Wind Player

Limits on available rehearsal time do not allow for complete drilling in rehearsals practicing holding long tones and lip slurs. Students must be taught to practice specific routines on a regular basis on their own. Establishing the importance of conscientious and consistent practice outside the band class on this specialized kind of routine is absolutely essential. Students must be made to realize that all it takes is one player who can't control the focus of the embouchure to destroy the sonority.

Instruction should begin in the earliest stages with beginning band students. From the first notes, a primary goal should be to stabilize the beginner embouchures. The method books do not include long tone drills. These drills have to be created by the director. A good routine is to hold each note twenty seconds, rest five seconds, and then hold the next note twenty seconds followed by the short rest, and so on.

Such a simple thing as establishing habits of consistently practicing long tones can spell the difference between mediocrity and outstanding musical results! Students must be convinced that the most boring exercise of all (long tones) can have the most significant beneficial results. Students must be taught to practice, on their own, the exercises that will build mature embouchures. It is ironic that there is very little published, either texts or specialized music drills, about this important aspect of playing. Consequently, the students must be taught how to make up their own practice routines and musical exercises that meet the specific needs in this area. Students should not only be taught how to develop stamina through proper conditioning exercises, they should also be taught how to care for their embouchures. This involves structured, carefully thought out playing exercises that consider exactly to what extent the embouchure is to be exercised and how much time should be allowed for resting. It's the play, rest, play, rest sequence that largely determines progress. Again, students must be taught why long tone practice is so important. The idea is not to make a "tough lip", but rather to allow accurate control and precision. It's the poise that makes the correct focus possible.

As I said before, players may continue to use the wrong embouchure for many years. Even advanced players may continue to play with a pinched or tight embouchure enduring years of endless playing problems. These players may think their embouchures are correct, but in fact, they are pinched. The problem is subtle and illusive. Many teachers, dealing with students on a day-to-day basis, observing many playing aspects of several individuals, may overlook the pinching problem. Embouchure pinching is the main cause of most intonation problems. An adjudicator will write, "Intonation problems persist and appear throughout the entire performance." That statement should cue you in to the fact that you have a problem with embouchure pinching. "Constant intonation problems" means players are playing with an incorrectly focused embouchure and are unable to adjust certain pitches. Remember, the pinched embouchure tires easily and has little endurance. Brass player struggle with high notes and notes are often "cuffed" or "burbled."

Attacks are often missed and there may be some struggle with articulations. Tone quality is generally bright and stuffy. Technique is slowed somewhat by a pinched embouchure.

Woodwind players who bite too much tire easily, develop chronic sore lips, suffer with intonation problems, have poor low register response, and a thin and sharp upper register. Several playing problems tend to exist together. If a player has one, he has several; the problems mentioned above are all interrelated.

Tone Drives

An effective variation of the long tone drill is to apply the pattern called tone drives. Long tones are practiced from very soft to very loud, sustained, and then diminished to soft again. Begin a note at the *pp* level, crescendo for four beats to the *ff* level, hold at the *ff* level for the same number of beats, then decrescendo the same number of beats back to *pp*. When proficiency is realized using the 4--4--4 pattern, then increase the specified number of beats in the routine to 5-- 5--5, then 6--6--6, etc. A reasonable goal for a young student is to be able to hold a long tone in a comfortable tessitura from twenty seconds to a full minute

Lip Slurs

For brass players, not only should their practice include conscientious effort on long tones and "tone drives", but it also must include equally important routines of lip slur patterns. Unfortunately, there is very little in print for the young student in the way of playing exercises or instruction. It's up to the band director or private teacher to make up these routines and show the student how to practice them.

Lip slurs should start using just two note patterns. Using valves 1,2,3, and progressing to valves 1,3, then 2,3, then 1,2, then 1, then 2, and finally to open, or no valves. Next, the slurs should involve three notes, then patterns using four notes, then five, then six and so on.

The "Squeeze Play"

The name, squeeze play, is a label for a certain variation of lip slur drills. This routine concentrates on building the body's breathing muscles as quickly as possible. After only a few days of practicing this routine the player will notice results. The routine: The final goal should be to reach the level of lip slur patterns that take a whole breath and continue until the player is almost out of air. For example, the player repeats, say, a three-note lip slur pattern without a break until almost out of air, then continues still without a break in the airflow holding the lowest tone of the pattern. When all the air is expelled, the player continues pushing for a couple of seconds even when there is no air left. The body may shake a little as the muscles are brought to maximum. These last few moments, although physically very demanding, offer the greatest benefit. The player should take about 20 seconds to rest after each of these demanding lip slur routines, then move up a half step and do the routine again. This segment of a practice session should last at least fifteen minutes. This developmental conditioning type of routine – the combination of lip slurs plus holding until there is absolutely no air left, then pushing a little more -- is a quick way to become an accomplished brass player in a short period of time.

Building stamina is the process of developing the necessary strength and control in the embouchure and breathing apparatus. It's the buildup of the body--all of the muscles and consequently strength--that it takes to play the instrument correctly. Long tone exercises and brass lip slurs should be a part of daily practice workouts.

Developing stamina must be included in the training of wind instrument players from the very first beginning stages.

Further Benefits of Proper Embouchure Focus:

Endurance

We educators seem to expect student embouchures to lack endurance. Students often tire before rehearsals and performances end. I have found that, without exception, student ensembles that have been trained for good sonority have no problem with endurance. They don't get tired because they are not fighting their instrument. They are tuned high enough that they can relax down to the pitch and don't have to lip up constantly! Playing with this approach allows student embouchures to endure with little effort during rehearsals and performances.

I experienced one example of this while observing a colleague who is one of the master high school band directors. He arranged for a recording company that had recently upgraded to new digital recording equipment to record his spring concert. The auditorium is noted for its fine acoustics so to take advantage of the digital equipment and fine acoustics; he scheduled a two-hour recording session for the afternoon before the concert. This session would allow a high quality digital recording to be made of the music the band had recently played at the State Festival. The program included the entire *Pictures at an Exhibition*, one of the most extensive and difficult pieces in band literature. The recording session was from 2:00 to 4:00 P.M. in the afternoon. For the concert that evening the program included *Capriccio Español*, Wagner's *Overture to The Flying Dutchman*, and the entire *Concerto for Two Trumpets* by Vivaldi. All are demanding and extensive works for band. At the end of local band concerts, it's the custom for band directors who have been in the audience to come to the stage to congratulate the director. As I approached, and before I could say anything, the director of this fine band leaned toward me and said, "See, they're not even tired. They could keep playing all night!" Immediately I knew what was going on in his mind! He was very much aware that endurance was not a problem for his band because he taught them the proper embouchure focus! He constantly reminds his students not to pinch and regularly emphasizes sonority at every rehearsal. [The director mentioned above is FBA Hall of Fame director Mr. Jack Crew].

Dynamics

Incidentally, this very well known and respected teacher is also noted for his use of very wide dynamics. His band's louds are very, very loud and without distortion while their softs are light and delicate. Remember, the statement that was made earlier: "The proper embouchure focus is like a panacea in curing the majority of problems in wind instrument playing." Using the proper embouchure focus enables the players to command a very wide range of dynamic levels from *ppp* to *fff* with control and without distortion.

Accuracy

One of the constant threats in wind instrument playing is the possibility of "cuffing" notes. Using the proper embouchure focus reduces the likelihood of distorted attacks. Brass players in particular will delight in finding they no longer 'blurble' notes. Woodwind players who learn not to bite will delight in increased low register response at all dynamic levels.

Range

Brass players will also find it easier to play in the high register when they use the proper embouchure focus. Brass teachers often stress that it isn't the tension in the lips that extends range as much as it is the speed of the air. So here is another "payoff' for using this system of embouchure focus.

Woodwind players will find the upper register tone will radically improve, and they will be able to control softer reeds thereby improving richness of tone and response in all registers. It becomes easier to execute light, delicate attacks and play with greater control, particularly in the softer dynamics. More control is possible at the extreme dynamics. All players can execute the softest pianissimo with precision and finesse. The louds can be played very loud without tonal distortion.

Intonation Deficiencies of Wind Instruments

We know that no instrument can be made to play perfectly 'in tune'; Players must learn to 'humor' bad notes--to lip the characteristically out of tune notes in tune. Every player must be made aware of the notes that are hard to play in tune and must be taught how to compensate for these irregularities.

Often the only instruction students get concerning intonation is being told they are out of tune. The teacher may point out places in the music that need attention but to be effective, instruction must go further. Students must be taught exactly how to play their instrument in tune. Telling students they are out of tune, telling them to listen and match pitches, etc., of course, is the correct thing to do, but merely telling them there is a problem is useless in correcting the problem if the students have not first been taught the proper embouchure focus. In fact, when the entire ensemble does use the correct focus, very little will need to be said about correcting intonation. The proper embouchure focus is a very big piece of the fine intonation and tone puzzle.

Review

1. The concept of embouchure focus must be thoroughly taught to all wind instrument players.

2. All students must be physically able to focus and poise the embouchure. This is arrived at through a carefully planned developmental program of stamina build-up called sonority drills.

3. All players must be taught to 'hear' where to focus the pitch and how to execute this ability in their playing.

4. Fine ensemble intonation is achieved when all players in an ensemble have mastered the proper embouchure focus. All it takes is one person who has no control to spoil the sonority.

Point #3 above, the ability of players to hear where to focus pitch, is the most difficult to achieve. It's been said, "Playing the horn is easy; hearing is the hard part." Good balance is critical to the development of fine sonority. Students cannot learn to hear across the ensemble if the instrumentation prohibits good balance. If the ensemble is top heavy with many flutes, clarinets, saxes, and trumpets with only a trombone or two, and only one tuba you have a big problem! The balance will be so 'top heavy' it will be impossible for anyone in the ensemble to hear well enough to be able to judge where to play in tune. Correct instrumentation is a must. Then everyone must be trained to hear across the entire ensemble.

In point #4 the proper embouchure focus is applied to achieve good intonation and a fine, characteristic tone quality.

- Left alone, almost all wind players will develop an incorrect, pinched embouchure.
- Most players retain a pinched embouchure throughout their entire school band career unless they are deliberately taught correct embouchure focus.
- The pinched embouchure is responsible for most playing problems.

- It is impossible for players to control their instrument without a focused embouchure.

Solos

When students play a solo in a band piece they play louder and often times will sound flat because their embouchure is more relaxed. In fact, it's this more relaxed embouchure that is the correct embouchure, the way they should have been playing all along. By using the proper embouchure focus, this common student error is eliminated.

• • •

Chapter 5: Buzzing

"Solfege- Sight sing- Buzz excerpts and studies."

--Adolph Herseth

We've established the importance of the properly focused embouchure. Now we must decide how to teach it to students. When students who have been playing for a long time with the wrong embouchure are first presented with the idea of the focused embouchure they often have trouble readjusting. In fact many players initially can't lip down. Even the most dedicated students (who will do anything they are asked to do) may have trouble learning to refocus their embouchures. Why? They lack the stamina necessary for the proper poise and focus. They don't yet have the physical control they need. However, they can develop these attributes quickly.

The key word here is stamina. Students need both stamina and control over all of the parts of the body that affect the breath and embouchure. Developing stamina does not mean building brute strength in the playing muscles. Although there is some physical development required, the goal should be learning to poise the muscles of the embouchure to the correct focus. Developing stamina does not mean building tough, rock-hard, inflexible muscles in the embouchure. Actually, quite the reverse is true. We are after an embouchure with relatively firm corners, but where the middle is both flexible and controlled...a centered embouchure which possesses the power to control its focus.

Special attention and specific time must be put forth in specialized instruction to develop stamina in all wind players. Day to day rehearsing of concert or marching music will not be enough to realize the desired results.

Many band directors do not realize the importance of developing the properly focused embouchure in each and every player. Consequently they do not take the time (nor do they use specialized materials) to develop this critical aspect of wind performance. Unfortunately their bands continue to be plagued with intonation, tone quality, and endurance problems.

The "Sing, Buzz, Blow" Technique

For brass players it's important to establish a mental picture of how the correct embouchure feels. They need to know how much embouchure tension to use. The "sing, buzz, blow" technique is a quick, sure way to teach the properly centered embouchure to brass players.

Sing

The player should first sing the note to be played in the middle range. You can use any one of many syllables: "Ah", "Lah", "Dah", "Doe." For trumpet players a good note to start with is second line G.

Buzz

Next have each player, using just the mouthpiece, buzz the note. At first he may have trouble lowering the pitch of the buzz down to the "G." This is the whole point of this technique. The player must learn to buzz the same pitch he is trying to play (in this case "G").

Blow

Then, when the buzz is stable and secure on the "G", have the player put the mouthpiece on the horn and play the note. The student may very well be shocked at how much better he sounds! You will be. It's a good idea to repeat the process several times until satisfied with the consistency. Next, have them use the "sing, buzz, blow" technique to play a tetrachord (e.g. "G, A, B, C" on trumpet).

Buzz the Music

Having the brass players practice buzzing entire sections of music is a great way to 1) solidify the centered tone and 2) train the inner ears of the musicians. Needless to say, this is excellent ear training!!! Be creative. Invent lip-slurring exercises and encourage the students to do the same at home.

Woodwinds

As mentioned earlier, student woodwind players often use too much bite pressure. A good exercise to improve this is to have them 1) puff their cheeks out and completely relax the embouchure while playing. Then 2) use the tongue to control the "honky" sound and 3) flatten the chin and cheeks **without** unnecessary pressure until the embouchure looks right. This teaches how the bite, tongue (oral cavity), and facial muscles work both independently and together. This is a very good exercise for use in sectionals and private lessons. The goal here is to teach proper relaxation without losing control of the tone.

• • •

Chapter 6: Dwelling

"I have learned that dwelling on sonorities – either unisons or chords – for several seconds (regardless of the written duration of the notes) helps students hear and produce better sonority."

--William C. Miller

For some decades researchers have reported that older and more experienced musicians consistently perform with more accurate intonation than younger performers (Geringer &Witt, 1985; Madsen, Edmonson, and Madsen, 1969; Platt & Racine, 1985; Worthy, 2000). It is also important to note that studies reveal other tendencies, including the tendency of experienced musicians to err in the direction of sharpness in both performance and perception tasks. Contemporary research has also suggested that both high school and college aged wind instrumentalists are not able to accurately discriminate mistunings of less than 10 cents in controlled paired pitch discrimination experiments (Clark, 2012). Furthermore, less experienced (non-professional) musicians may be adversely affected by the demands inherent in the process of performing on an instrument (Duke, 1985; Madsen, Edmonson, & Madsen, 1969).

Whatever the causes, teenage students seem to take a longer time than adults to hear sonorities clearly. It may be that the interactions between the brain and the sensory organs (both seeing and hearing) are different in teenage students than in adults. Perhaps teens require longer periods of concentration to be able to fully recognize tone and pitch and then produce good sonority. Related research revealed that junior high aged students could learn to accurately tune unisons and intervals when trained to recognize beats and given adequate time to perform the task (Miles, 1972). I have learned that dwelling on sonorities -- either unisons or chords -- for several seconds (regardless of the written duration of the notes) helps students hear and produce better sonority. This technique of dwelling on individual chords works, improving pitch and sonority. Perhaps it works because it gives students enough time to individually recognize pitch problems and then make proper adjustments.

One good dwelling exercise is to simply play passages very slowly, allowing each chord to sound for several seconds, regardless of the written value. Students may at first consider this a very boring procedure -- taking several minutes to play a very few notes – but proof of the value of this technique is at hand. The simple act of explaining to students why dwelling is important seems to eliminate much, if not all boredom. If you convince the students that dwelling is a "secret weapon" they will much more readily buy-in to the process. After dwelling on the sonorities in one section of the music for a while, return immediately to the beginning of that section and play it up to tempo. The students will almost certainly notice a significant improvement in the sonority and intonation of the ensemble. Once they experience this excellent sonority they will want to continue with the technique until they can consistently capture it and make the music "sound" at all times. In the early stages of learning the process "dwelling" usually takes ten seconds or more on each note regardless of the printed value of the note. Be patient.

A common practice for directors is to use chorales as warm-ups. I have learned that even these notes go by too fast to give players time to listen and adjust. To more effectively teach sonority, drills must be devised that allow the band to dwell on each unison or chord note. Another effective ensemble drill is to play unison scales, holding each tone for twenty seconds. Even a scale of four count whole notes at mm = 60 does not allow enough dwelling time on each tone. Understand that while dwelling drills help develop stamina, at some point they become quite tedious musically. When the process becomes too tedious it is better to break off and play the music in real time just to recapture the musical qualities. "Sell" the group on the importance of a professional tone and all its benefits. Before long everyone will notice much better intonation and tone quality because of dwelling drills. An excellent by-product of dwelling on sonorities for long periods of time is that it is also a great opportunity for students to work on improving embouchure focus.

• • •

Chapter 7: Projection and the Performance Environment

"I know the price of success: dedication, hard work and an unremitting devotion to the things you want to see happen."

--Frank Lloyd Wright

Day after day, meeting in the confines of a rehearsal room, ensembles tend to let down in the areas of tonal intensity and projection. Bands tend to play only to the walls directly in front of them and only fill the rehearsal room with sound. Conscious effort must be made to help the players learn to overcome this tendency and its limitations. The ensemble director may ask each player to imagine they are on an auditorium stage and to 'play to the back of the hall'...but this is only a partial solution.

It is wise to move certain rehearsals out of the confines of the rehearsal room and onto the stage of an auditorium. In the auditorium environment, special focus can be directed to tonal projection. All this, of course, involves dealing with breath support, balance, and the observation of correct dynamics while asking for tonal projection. But I must emphasize here that giving careful attention to tonal projection can greatly affect a band's sonority.

Improving Your Perspective with the Help of a Colleague

While in the auditorium, it's also wise to examine the band's performance from the perspective of the audience. A good way to do this is to call on a colleague to conduct a portion (or portions) of the auditorium rehearsal. This allows you a chance to move back in the audience to hear from that vantage point. Armed with a note pad, pencil, and scores, this is a wonderful opportunity to listen and make notes on what to change in follow-up rehearsals. This experience is often a very revealing and you will probably find many specific spots that need attention and alteration. This process can make a great deal of difference in the band's future performances.

· · ·

Chapter 8: Step-Up Mouthpieces

A significant improvement in the sonority of a band can be achieved by having students "step up" to mouthpieces designed for professional playing. This is absolutely essential if the group is to realize the finest quality sonority. Most mouthpieces that come with the student model instruments are intended for beginners…young students. As student players mature, they should step-up to a mouthpiece that is more like what a 'professional player' would use. Ideally this 'step-up' should happen around the 8th grade. The changeover should be completed at least by January of the 9th grade year. It's important for every player (not just the best ones) to make the "step-up." A significant improvement in the overall tone quality of the ensemble will occur when all players make the change. This is a very important factor in developing a superior band sound.

The following recommendations are my own. Mouthpieces of similar dimensions can be found in several brands. It's the responsibility of the band director to let students know about stepping up. Every student in a section should be encouraged to play on the same type mouthpiece so everyone will get the same basic tone quality. Many professional orchestra sections play on matching equipment for a reason!

Mouthpiece Recommendations:

- Bb clarinet - Vandoren B-45 using #3 Vandoren reeds
- Saxes - Selmer LT or Vandoren AL3 mouthpiece using #3 Vandoren reeds (or softer)
- Trumpets - Bach 3C
- Trombone and baritone - Bach 6½ AL
- Tuba - the smaller of the two models of Helleburg tuba mouthpieces.

Several manufacturers make mouthpieces with similar dimensions under their name and system of sizing. The brass mouthpiece dimensions mentioned get a big, dark sound, and they work well for the concert band. Avoid shallow brass mouthpieces; it's a fallacy to think it's necessary to play on a small mouthpiece to get higher notes in the concert band setting.

It is important for the sax section of the jazz band to use "jazz" model mouthpieces. The Selmer LT, the Selmer CS-80, the Vandoren AL3 and those of similar size allow for an excellent 'classical' sax sound, but they don't have the "kick" needed for jazz. For serious jazz band work the jazz model mouthpiece is necessary. I suggest ordering a set of Meyer MM-6 mouthpieces as a starting point. Get 2 alto, 2 tenor, and 1 bari mouthpiece. Then issue these band owned mouthpieces to the players (if each player can't arrange to furnish their own mouthpiece). [When students are ready to buy their own mouthpiece the Beechler Diamond Inlay and Claude Lakey jazz alto saxophone mouthpieces are superb and the Guardala "King" tenor and Otto Link bari mouthpieces are excellent as well. With all jazz sax mouthpieces it is best to either try them out or aim for medium sizes. Remember, jazz saxophone mouthpieces have a larger tip opening and almost always require a softer reed. Hard reeds are NOT macho. They are often counterproductive.]

• • •

Chapter 9: Nilo Hovey Clinic: Tuning the Clarinet and the Band

One of the finest, most rewarding clinics I ever attended was a presentation on tuning the clarinet and using it as the pitch standard for tuning the rest of the band by Nilo Hovey, member of The National Band Association Hall of Fame and author of the *"T-I-P-P-S for Band"* series. As I mentioned in the Preface I worked the large five-week band camp at the University of Miami for many years. In addition to our regular staff, Fred McCall made it a practice to bringing in various outstanding band people for special one week stays. One summer Nilo Hovey was one of those special people. I remembered hearing his outstanding clinic before, so I asked Mr. Hovey if I could record it to share with others. He was delighted to be recorded and made a special effort to do a spectacular job that day. The following is a transcript of that clinic presentation. He used four junior-high aged clarinet playing band campers for demonstration. All statements below are from Mr. Hovey unless otherwise indicated.

The Clinic

There are five steps in establishing fine intonation in a band

1. A pitch standard must be used that is attainable by all of the instruments. A-440 is the best standard to use. If 444 were used, there would be some instruments that would not be able to reach that level. If 438 were used, all would be able to get down to pitch, but some would distort their own sound to achieve this.

2. An efficient method must be used that allows each instrument to tune to the standard pitch level. Special attention must be given to those instruments that have the least flexibility in tuning. In every instance these are the woodwind instruments. Brass instruments can make a

wider variation of pitch level than the woodwinds. The most efficient method of tuning means that tuning must involve more than one note. Just tuning to Bb concert alone is not enough. In fact, using only this one note can be detrimental.

3. Each player must be taught the intonation deficiencies of his particular instrument. For example, 4th line D on the alto sax tends to be sharp, 4th space E on the trumpet tends to be flat.

4. Once all players know the exceptional notes on their Instruments, then each one must be taught how to "humor" the bad notes and bring them in tune. The method is not always the same. For example, a flute player changes the direction of the air column. If the pitch is high, the air is blown more into the tone hole to bring the pitch down. A French horn player changes the position of the hand in the bell. It's the simplest for a trombone player; he just moves the slide a little.

5. Enough time must be provided in each rehearsal to allow each player to hear his own instrument in relation to the total ensemble. If done correctly, this should result in a long-range process of ear training and a continuing, never-ending process of refinement and reevaluation of the intonation of the ensemble.

When we tune the band, we must do more than just set a machine to give a pitch standard. We must constantly be training the students to do their own listening and must teach them how to adjust on their particular instrument. The ultimate goal is for all players to be able to perfectly match on their own and play with excellent intonation.

The pitch standard should be established around the clarinet section. The reason is the clarinet, over any other instrument, is the least flexible when it comes to altering its pitch level. Charles Righter in his book *Success in Teaching: School Orchestras and Bands* (Righter, 1955) emphasizes establishing a "pitch conscious nucleus" that centers on the woodwind quintet within the band. Get that quintet in tune, and then use it to establish the pitch standard for the rest of the band. This is a good idea, but we must start by getting the clarinet in tune with itself.

In the case of the clarinet: When we pull the barrel (not the mouthpiece going into the barrel), we find it affects some notes more than others. The throat tone notes, which include bottom line Eb up to middle line Bb are flattened much more than the long tube notes such as middle line B natural up to around top line F. All notes are affected by pulling the barrel, and the long tube notes are affected the least. There may be a student or two that can't come up to pitch because of a poor embouchure or poor reed. It is important not to sacrifice the A-440 standard because of these weaker students. Special effort must be taken to work with just these students to correct their embouchure and get them on a medium firm reed. Many directors have students use number 2½ reeds. A better choice would be around a 3 or even 3½ and work intensely with the weak students to bring them up to standard as quickly as possible.

Using F concert -- open G on the clarinet -- bring the entire section as close as possible to this pitch standard.

As was mentioned above, it is a good practice to tune to more than one note. A convenient chord to use is the Bb concert triad -- the C major chord on the clarinet. Check the bottom line E. If it is flat, then the barrel must be pushed in a little to bring it up to pitch. Remember, flat notes can't be raised, but lipping down can lower sharp notes. Next, check third space C and top space E. If these notes are sharp, then pull the middle joint a little to bring them down.

There are two cases where this can't be done:

1. If the clarinet has an 'articulated' G sharp, or

2. If any notes from middle line B up to A flat above the staff are already flat, then pulling would only make things worse by making flat notes more flat.

3. Clarion register notes must sometimes be lipped down if they are sharp. Students should be taught to do this by:

- Bringing in the corners of the mouth
- By dropping the lower jaw slightly
- By getting a larger oral cavity -- getting a larger "ah" feeling inside the mouth

(More recent research by Mr. Raymond Wheeler using fluoroscope technology has shown that professional woodwind players actually raise the tongue for the lower notes and lower the tongue for notes in the higher register (Wheeler, 2010)!

Cross Tuning

It isn't enough to get just one note in tune. By using the notes of the C major triad, three notes at a time can be checked. (The book *Section Studies for Bb Clarinets* was written by Hovey and addresses this approach to tuning. Chords are built by pyramiding so each pitch can be heard more easily (Hovey, ca. 1950). Constantly be checking the pitch of the "long tube notes" against the pitch of the "short tube notes." The same can be applied to the saxophone. Pulling the mouthpiece lowers the notes of the left hand compared to the right hand. Pushing in the mouthpiece raises the left hand notes more than the right hand notes. (Remember, it is always better to lip down on any wind instrument than to lip up.)

The Hovey book allows for students to switch parts. 3rds can play 1st, 2nds on the 3rd, etc. This allows all students to hear from every perspective. Note: This switching of parts is possible for all the instruments in drills provided in Fussell's *Exercises for Ensemble Drill* (Fussell, 1985).

Question: Our tuning standard of A-440 is based on a room temperature of 72 degrees. What do we do when the temperature reaches as high as 90 degrees which is frequently found in Florida weather or the summer months in the northern states?

Answer: All of the wind instruments drift up in pitch together, some more than others. If only wind instruments are playing together, then the easiest solution is to allow the pitch standard to change and still use the clarinet as the pitch standard. Get all of the clarinets in tune with themselves, and then tune the rest of the band to the clarinets. The real problem comes when wind instruments have to play with mallets at these temperatures. Temperature extremes don't affect the mallets nearly as much as wind instruments. At a higher temperature, allowing all winds to tune to themselves as mentioned, the mallets will sound quite flat. Actually, it's the winds that have gone sharp.

Dealing with Certain Notes

- Is there ever a time when the bell joint is moved? Only middle line B and low E are affected. Usually these are of no concern. If a B is a little sharp, it can be lipped down a little. If the B is flat, rock the first finger over and open the throat A key while still covering the hole for B. This tends to raise the B a little.

- Generally the only notes lowered by putting on more fingers are the throat tone notes (g, g#, a, a#). To lower them, put all the fingers down in the right hand.

- Not much can be done with low E and F. We get into a slightly sharp register around low A and B; they are easy to lip down. Eb and E might be low if the instrument is not tuned correctly. If they are low, using the C# key can raise them. F and G can be raised by opening one of the side keys. The main goal is to set the barrel so these notes are in tune. Top space E tends to be low, but the Eb key can be opened to raise this area.

- "Venting" refers to opening certain keys only to raise a certain flat pitch. Venting is used only when there is a sustained note and we want to get it very well in tune. When we get up to around high B, C, and C# we are in a sharp register of the clarinet.

- Many professional players do not want a horn that is in tune on a high C. Probably they have been playing for so long on instruments tuned that way they don't feel right if octave Cs are in tune. Also, there is something about the design of the clarinet that allows a better response if the horn is tuned that way. It's no problem to make a horn that is perfectly in tune on a high C, but it's what that does to the rest of the horn that counts.

- High C# is already a sharp note so don't use the Eb vent key on this note. Instead, start using the Eb vent key on D and above.

- Be sure to have a reed trimmer, "Dutch rush", or very fine sandpaper. Also, an automobile body file can be used to shave the back of the reed and provide a perfectly flat surface to go against the table of the mouthpiece. Go to an auto parts store and buy an auto body file with 10 teeth to the inch. It will cost about $30 (it will be more than that today). Filing the reed gently (and flat) against the teeth will make a perfectly flat surface that will seal better against the table of the mouthpiece.

The Mystery of the Squeaking Clarinets, Part One

(Hovey was asked about students developing persistent squeaking on the clarinet after about three years of playing when up until then they had had no trouble. His answer was most revealing.)

Student clarinets come with a plastic mouthpiece that is made by molding molten plastic. During the molding process the molten plastic is compressed. Over a period of time the plastic swells and wants to return to its natural state. When this happens the table of the mouthpiece may develop a slight warp. This unevenness causes many squeaks. The solution is simple. Have students specify a high quality hard rubber mouthpiece when purchasing their clarinet.

• • •

Chapter 10: A Routine for Tuning the Band

A Tuning Philosophy

The tuning adjustment of all wind instruments should follow a philosophy of tuning that will allow performers the latitude to adjust pitches in order to correct intonation problems. There is very little latitude when trying to lip up; it is almost impossible. However there is a great deal of leeway to lip down. On some instruments, saxophone for example, it's possible to lip down more than one-half step. On saxophone many players tend to be sharp in the upper register due to too much bite pressure. Saxophonists should always tune the instrument to a convenient note in the middle register. This way the flattest notes on the instrument are tuned up to pitch and upper register sharp notes may be easily lipped down. The player will find a focused, correctly formed and relaxed embouchure, with a minimum of "biting," and a mouthpiece which is **pushed in far enough** allows the saxophone, with only slight variations, to be played quite well in tune.

Tuning up should be a very carefully planned procedure that need not take an excessive amount of time. Once established, tuning need only take a few seconds. Some make tuning a mindless ritual. As a judge I have observed many bands playing a Bb concert scale during warm-up at festival **with not one person** making any attempt to change the tuning of their instrument! Tuning should be a constant consideration in any musical ensemble, not a mindless ritual. A pitch reference should be given from time to time during rehearsal, but players must learn to attend to their own tuning at all times.

It is better to wait until all the instruments have had a chance to warm up. Larger instruments are more affected by temperature change so their tuning is particularly critical. Constantly check to make sure the pitch is not allowed to drift upward as they warm up.

The worst time to tune is at the beginning of the rehearsal because many wind instruments are not yet warmed up.

Consider this: The overtones of the large low sounding wind instruments are in the range of the fundamental notes of the upper instruments. The upper voices will seem flat if the lower voices are sharp and their overtones are beating against the fundamentals of the upper voices instead of resonating with them. Therefore the lower voices must always be kept down to the A = 440 Hz pitch standard.

It is critical to remember that it is nearly impossible for the oboes, clarinets and bassoons to play much above A = 440 Hz while brass and saxophone players can push in if the pitch rises. The double reeds and clarinets are the first to suffer when the pitch of the ensemble rises above A = 440 Hz. The tendency is for the pitch to creep up as the ensemble plays and the instruments warm. Again, it is very important for the tuning standard to be held to the A=440 Hz standard. Constant attention must be given to tuning during rehearsals and performances and all players, particularly the low voices, must learn to keep the pitch down to the standard.

Traditional tuning notes should be avoided when they are not practical. For example, tuning only to Bb concert, or using the oboe's "A" are poor choices for tuning winds. "A", is a good note for tuning the strings in orchestras, but this doesn't serve the winds well. They should be tuned to notes that reveal the true tuning of the wind instruments. "F" concert above middle "C" is a very practical note to use for all wind instruments in the band, except alto, baritone sax and oboe, and Bb concert is fine for brasses. Use Bb and F as a minimum.

Definition of Concert Pitch

The term concert pitch means a pitch that is "in sound", i.e. the note on the keyboard without transposition. For example, "F concert" on the keyboard is played as a "G" on the Bb clarinet and is a "D" on the alto sax. Teach students the basic transpositions for their instruments. It is important.

Electronic Tuners

Modern technology has made a number of very accurate tuners available. Strobe-based tuners, quartz oscillator based electronic tuners, and tuning apps on cell phones and other personal computing devices all get the job done quite well and are a must for obtaining an accurate pitch reference. But be aware that the strobe tuners and the audio and metered electronic tuners show pitches that are mathematical multiples. For example, on these devices the octaves of A=440 Hz are: 55, 110, 220, 440, 880, 1760, etc. However, this is not the way the human ear hears. The human ear wants to hear what are called "stretched" octaves in the more extreme ranges, flatter as notes go lower and sharper as notes go higher. In other words, with A=440, the ear will hear 55 Hz as sharp and 1760 Hz as flat. So follow the tendency of the human ear to hear in this way. Never use a tuner on piccolo or flute in upper octaves!

A practical approach is to set the tuner only to notes near A = 440 to establish a pitch standard, then tune the instruments by ear after that. Avoid using the tuner's meter on very high and very low pitches and avoid sounding the tuner in these ranges as well. Sounding the tuner in its middle range and tuning by ear will automatically help compensate for the stretched octave effect.

Wind Instruments Are Not Built Perfectly "In Tune"

It is impossible to build wind instruments that play perfectly "in tune." Keyboard instruments when tuned will hold their tuning, but wind instruments must be compensated, "lipped" or "humored" in some way to get them to play in tune. They must be tuned so that it is within the ability of the player to bring all notes into tune by adjusting in some way. It is important to keep in mind that on all wind instruments it is difficult if not impossible to adjust a pitch up, but it is quite easy to adjust down to bring a pitch in tune.

All wind instruments produce a *natural* or *Pythagorean* overtone series. This lies in contrast to the fact that keyboard, mallet, and electronic keyboard instruments are all tuned to the *equal tempered* tuning system. In essence the *equal tempered* system ignores the *Pythagorean* system of tuning each note based on mathematical ratios. Instead it divides each octave into 12 equal-sized half steps. Therefore, in order to play in tune with mallets and keyboards it becomes even more important for wind instrumentalists to be able to listen and adjust each pitch by ear.

The Effects of Temperature

Today our wind instruments are built to play their best at 72 degrees using the pitch standard of A=440 Hz. Problems arise when the environmental temperatures vary, either above or below the ideal of 72 degrees. Acoustical keyboard instruments are not affected much by temperature extremes but wind instruments are. Body heat and the heat from lighting may cause the temperature in a rehearsal or concert to rise. This causes the larger, low wind instruments to rise more than the smaller instruments. The tubas, if allowed, will go quite sharp making the smaller instruments sound flat. The bass voices set the pitch level because of their position in the overtone structure. If they are sharp, it aggravates conditions in the smaller instruments and creates problems:

1. Embouchure tensions increase and students move away from the proper embouchure focus discussed earlier.

2. The available tuning leeway is disturbed, particularly for the woodwind instruments. Solution: If possible, stick to 72 degrees and make tuning corrections throughout rehearsals and concerts, being particular to keep the low and mid voices down to standard. Note: Pianos and mallets do go slightly flat as the temperature rises, and pipe organs go sharp.

Pottle (1966) says: "Tuning sharp of the standard A=440 Hz is a most unfortunate intonation error and is committed by many instrumental organizations." It is usually caused by inattention to warm up and not using a reliable reference pitch.

The Pitch Standard under Extreme Temperatures

If only wind instruments are involved under extreme temperature conditions, such as a performance outdoors in the cold, it is better to conform to the pitch level that the extreme temperature dictates. Practical experience has shown that bands play much better in tune under adverse temperature conditions by following this than trying to stay with the A=440 Hz standard.

The best pitch reference to use in the band is the first chair clarinet player. Reason: The tuning adjustment on all of the other wind instruments is not as critical as on the clarinet because the clarinet is the least flexible when it comes to lipping up or down (See Nilo Hovey clinic notes, Chapter 8). Also, because there are many clarinets in a band, it is wise to get that section in tune with itself, and then tune the rest of the band to the clarinets.

Oboes and Bassoons are Special

Do not follow the tradition of using the oboe as the pitch standard in tuning. Correct tuning for the oboe and bassoon depends on the way the reeds are cut. If these instruments are flat they can be brought up to pitch only by adjusting (shaving and/or cutting) the reed. Also, oboe and bassoon are more affected by embouchure tension and therefore may provide a less reliable tuning pitch than the clarinet.

The "Coin Trick"

A Selmer company clarinet (Bundy or Signet) can be brought close to being in tune with itself by pulling the barrel the thickness of a nickel coin. A Leblanc company clarinet (Vito, Normandy, or Noblet) will be close when the barrel is pulled the thickness of a dime. Teaching clarinet students to use the "coin trick" for tuning will get them in the ballpark. Remember, clarinets are made to be played with the barrel pulled unless some special barrel is being used that avoids the gap.

How to Use the Clarinet as the Pitch Standard

Have the top player sound their C major arpeggio slowly starting on written middle C. See if the bottom line E and second line G are in tune. If they are sharp, pull the barrel; if they are flat, push the barrel in. In extreme cases it may be necessary to pull a clarinet at the middle joint to bring down the notes of the right hand. For example, 3rd space "C" may be sharp to middle "C" and pulling at the middle joint may help. When the top chair player is in tune with himself, use him as the "standard", and check out the rest of the clarinet section.

Watch out for the weak player who seems to be flat. The problem may be caused by a very soft reed. Often, however, it's caused by too little bite, the wrong oral cavity shape, and/or lack of support. Always be careful not to let reed players bite too much, just enough to get the pitch up to the 440 standard. Insist every player always use a proper mouthpiece, a reed that matches the mouthpiece, and a proper embouchure. In fact, without everyone in the clarinet and sax section using the proper strength reed (matched to their mouthpiece) and a correct embouchure there is little likelihood they can play in tune or get a good tone.

All it takes is one careless player to destroy the sonority of ensemble.

Recommended Tuning Routine

Remember, it is not wise to tune just once at the beginning of a rehearsal. This is actually the worst time to tune. Wait until the large instruments are warm. A good time to tune is several minutes into a rehearsal possibly after the first selection. Remember, large instruments change more than small ones as they warm up and they take longer to warm up. Ask the students to make sure their slide/mouthpiece/ barrel/head joint is in the normal position. Then proceed from there.

It may be necessary to tune more than once during rehearsals and performances just as professional orchestras do. A conductor must constantly be aware of the variable forces that may be affecting the tuning of the band such as air conditioning, the heat from stage lighting, the room heating up from so much body heat from the players, etc. It is a good idea to have a thermometer mounted on the wall near the podium in the rehearsal room.

Always tune the marching band just before the outdoor performance. The temperature can vary considerably from day to day and must be taken into consideration.

Students must be taught to have their instrument warm when they tune. It is useless to tune before the instrument and embouchure are warmed up and ready. It is interesting to note that it is not the temperature of the material of the instruments, but the temperature of the air inside the instrument that affects tuning. Of course, the air inside is affected by the temperature of the material (metal or wood), but the material itself does not change length or shape at different temperatures more than a few microns.

The Routine:

1. Check the top chair Bb clarinets to make sure they are in tune with themselves where the notes at the long tube (third space C) are in tune with those at the short tube (open G) then check with the electronic tuner to confirm.

2. Next tune the rest of the clarinet section using the open G (F concert) on the instrument. Check bottom line E (D concert) if big discrepancies appear. Sometimes this is a better note to use. Impress on all woodwind players that they must think in terms of "short tube notes" and "long tube notes" and to check each end of their instrument when tuning.

3. Tune the flutes using low or middle F because it's in the middle of the tube. Do not use Bb; it is very sharp on a flute. When only Bb is used, flute players tend to pull out too much. This is such a common fault found in many bands. I facetiously call it "the flat flute syndrome."

4. Use F for oboe and bassoon, keeping in mind that if a player can't come up to pitch the reed needs adjustment.

5. Tune the tenor sax on their low G. Never tune saxophones in the upper register; it's slightly sharp to the lower register. Teach sax players to tune to their low register and lip down the upper register. (The sharp upper register is exaggerated when students play with too much bite pressure.)

6. Tune the French horn using F concert, but come back to them later using Bb concert.

7. At this point, switch to Bb concert as the pitch standard using the top chair Bb clarinet player or the electronic tuner. Check to see if the clarinet player maintained the same spot on the electronic tuner.

8. Tune alto and baritone saxophones. Use their low G. Again, avoid tuning saxophones to their upper register notes.

9. Tune trumpets, trombones, baritones, tubas, and horns next using the Bb concert.

Stretched Octaves

As I said before, be aware that the human ear hears what are called "stretched octaves." This is a human perception phenomenon that is still not fully understood. The ear wants to hear very low notes flatter and very high notes sharper than the way they register on an electronic tuner where octaves are in the ratios of 1:2:4:8:16, etc. In other words, at A = 440 Hz when the tuba shows 10 to 15 cents flat and the piccolo shows 10 to 15 cents sharp the ear hears them both as being "in tune."

In practical application this means DO NOT use the electronic tuner to tune the extreme ranges. Do not use the electronic tuner to tune piccolos, flutes, or clarinets in the upper register, or tubas, baritone saxes, etc., in the low register. Tune them by ear.

Do not sound an extremely high or low tone on an electronic tuner for matching. The correct way to use an electronic tuner is to sound the tuning tone in the range around middle C, then let the players compare their tones 'by ear.' If the meter is used, only tune to pitches in the middle C range.

Visual Tuning Versus Aural Tuning

Do not take the time to show each player the meter on an electronic tuner during the ensemble tuning process. While some research has shown an improvement in tuning accuracy in subjects who underwent specific intonation training using visual feedback (Platt and Racine, 1985), the key word here is training. Showing them the dial once at the beginning of rehearsals or performances is not the same as providing repeated trials in a designed training program. It is good to train them how to use the tuner to make sure they are up to the A = 440 Hz pitch standard and to find the intonation tendencies of certain notes during their own private practice sessions. Wickes recommends pairing students up and using an electronic tuner along with a tuning test to teach them the intonation tendencies of their particular instruments (Wickes, 1990). This is a very good technique for use in private lessons and private practice sessions. But the tuning process before performances and rehearsals is not the time to show student the tuner dial. By then, it's too late. First and foremost you want to train them to set their instrument's tuning apparatus and where, and to whom, they need to listen.

Where to Listen

Many of us have heard clinicians and other directors direct ensemble members to "listen down" or "listen to the tubas" on numerous occasions. Balancing the ensemble so that the low voices are stronger than the highest voices is an important foundation of good ensemble balance because the higher pitched instruments sound louder. McBeth wrote an entire booklet on this topic (McBeth, 1972) and directors should certainly strive to maintain good ensemble balance at all times. However, the question of who the players should listen to in the ensemble is much more complicated. First of all, McBeth's approach advocates balancing to the lowest voices, not necessarily listening to, or tuning to, the lowest voices. Tuning to the tuba is a topic ripe for further investigation (See Byo, Schlegel, and Clark, 2011). Secondly, it is not always possible to hear the lowest voice(s) while other instruments are playing. It is not reasonable to expect students sitting in front of the trumpet or trombone section to hear much other than the relatively loud sounds playing behind their heads! The many orchestra and military band players I have asked over the years have all told me that they listen to several different pitch references while playing:

1. The players who share their melodic or contrapuntal line or the same chord tone

2. The players closest to them (and behind them!)

3. The players in their octave

4. Players mirroring their part in other octaves

5. The chord fundamental (bass) when present

Perhaps a more fruitful approach would be to train every student to listen actively to their own tone and tuning and compare it to everything they can hear at all times! Yes, it is a lot to ask.

Teenage Brain Reaction Time

While much auditory research measures brain reaction times in milliseconds, I have found that teenaged musicians need several seconds to actually "hear" a reference pitch. It is a good practice to teach students to wait three seconds before testing their tuning. Teach students to stop playing if they can't hear the pitch standard and play only when they are able to hear the pitch standard and can compare.

Sounding the Pitch Routine

1. Sound the pitch standard

2. Allow time to tune

3. Repeat this process back and forth about four times until everyone is sure of their tuning

Adopt the Focus Concept for Sonority

Teach tuning through the concept of "focusing" the embouchure to pitch. Remember, it isn't possible to lip up as much as it is to lip down, so focusing really means setting the equipment to lip down, not up.

Drifting Sharp

Remember that an ensemble of wind instrumentalists will have a tendency to drift sharp as they warm up. It is up to the conductor to keep the pitch standard down to A=440. Watch the low voices in particular.

Summary

Often, we observe bands with good precision, reading skills, and tone quality, but because of poor intonation their otherwise fine performance is destroyed. For student wind players the most difficult and often unmastered aspect of playing seems to be hearing the entire ensemble. Those who can't hear are unable to play in tune or achieve good balance and blend because they have not acquired the necessary hearing skills. Students must be rehearsed and taught to hear and must be taught how to compensate for the intonation discrepancies of their individual instruments. Remember, as mentioned earlier, being able to compensate is mostly a matter of building up the stamina to being able to focus and poise the embouchure holding to a centered pitch. Students must be taught how to build their stamina and master the ability to focus and hold a pitch center. This ability comes from everyone practicing long tones and tone drives, and from brass players practicing lip slurs. There is not enough time to adequately drill in the rehearsal situation, so students must be trained to practice in the private setting at home where more time can be devoted to the physical conditioning necessary to build stamina.

Some attention must be given in rehearsals to drilling long tone unison scales in order to train students what to do at home. Also, a director must make it a major project to drill the band in memorizing all of the major scales. This serves several purposes:

1. Students who know their scales tend to play fewer wrong notes

2. Scales also benefit technical facility. Those who have mastered their scales can handle difficult runs and sight reading better

3. When individuals already know scale interval "steps", they can use this familiarity as a pitch reference aid to teach themselves.

Important Rehearsal Resources

- Fussell, Raymond C. (1985). Exercises *for Ensemble Drill*. Los Angeles: Alfred Publishing Company, Inc. [This is one of the few publications that take players through all keys and scales. Every book is identical and can be used by all instruments at one time. I consider this book and the Treasury of Scales (Smith, 1980) as must-haves for complete ensemble drills.]

- Smith, Leonard B. (1980). *Treasury of Scales*. Miami: Belwin, Inc.
- Sueta, Ed, (1985). Rhythm Vocabulary Chart Volume One. Rockaway, NJ: Ed Sueta Music. Great for teaching and reviewing counting and rhythm reading
- Pottle, Ralph R. (1966). *Tuning the School Band and Orchestra*. Hammond, Louisiana: Ralph R. Pottle.
- Stauffer, Donald (1987). Intonation Deficiencies of Wind Instruments in Ensemble. Birmingham, AL: Donald Stauffer.

• • •

Chapter 11: The Monolithic Band Sound
Scoring Practices Then and Now

The Finlandia Year

Some years ago I had a unique experience. My Lakeland High School band was doing well. The program was large and the junior high bands were sending students that were very well prepared. Over 100 sophomores a year could be expected and they could sight read grade three music!

For festival, I picked Claude Smith's *Symphony No.1*, a hard piece but accessible. For the second big number I chose an old favorite, *Finlandia*. I had not had an opportunity to work it before, so I welcomed the challenge. I knew my Symphonic Band could easily handle the piece. I remembered that one of our guest conductors, Paul Lavalle, did *Finlandia* with the University of Miami Band when I was a member. He visited Miami and did a remote with our band on his NBC radio program, "The Band of America." Later, Henry Fillmore went to New York to guest host Lavalle's band for the broadcast. This was during the last of "big time" radio, 1953.

At State Festival, we received "superior" ratings from all three judges, but I was surprised when two of the three judges criticized the sound of the band in *Finlandia*. One judge only talked about the overly big sound, but the other judge talked about the "monolithic" sound. He said we sounded too big and heavy all the time and called it the monolithic sound. I was puzzled.

These comments struck me as odd at the time, and I had other pressing matters at the moment. Some weeks later, I decided to try to find out what these two judges found objectionable, so I took the scores, the judges' comment sheets, and the judges' tape recorded comments home. I sat down with a pad and pencil and started listening intently. What was this "monolithic" sound? The answer was almost immediately apparent. The older transcription of *Finlandia* was very much over-scored. It was obvious that there was a lot of doubling, and when I took a closer look at the individual parts I realized that everyone was playing most of the time. Listening to *Finlandia* in its original form as an orchestra piece confirmed my suspicions. What the one judge called the "monolithic" sound of the band was actually the big, monotonous sound of constant full scoring.

A conductor today who has the opportunity to work both older and newer band literature immediately realizes that the older pieces are scored in a way that keeps everyone playing almost constantly. Today's modem composers may have individual players resting through as much as one third of a piece. Further examination of older arrangements and original music from several decades ago revealed that full scoring was the accepted way to score at that time. Today, we find composers and arrangers using a greater variety of scoring textures and colors. Today, there is less doubling, particularly in the more advanced pieces.

The Egmont Overture Episode

Several years had passed when a colleague sent me the District Festival performance recording of his band playing Beethoven's *Egmont* Overture. The playing was excellent, and they had received a "superior" rating at the District Festival (allowing the band to go on to State Festival a few weeks later). The band director wanted my opinion. He knew there were problems with the performance.

Yes, there was one major big problem. Immediately after listening to the recording I picked up the phone and called him with this advice: The band was going to "crash and burn" if he played *Egmont* at State. My advice was that *Egmont* was a poor selection, the arrangement was too thickly scored, and for him to change to a different number. He insisted it was too late for that and he had to stick with *Egmont*.

What to do? Then I remembered my episode with *Finlandia* and realized that the problem was the same. *Egmont* was too over-scored for contemporary performance. That kind of scoring might be appropriate for playing at an outdoor concert when everything had to be big and full, but certainly not for State Festival. There was only one solution. If the band had to stick with *Egmont*, my advice was to fix the arrangement. Like many earlier transcriptions, this one came with just a two line score. There was no way to know what all of the parts were doing without a full score. It would be a lot of work, but the only way to proceed was to build a complete full score by referencing all of the parts.

Next, we needed to get a copy of the original Beethoven orchestral score and a definitive orchestral recording. Then, using those as a reference, we needed to edit the band transcription, taking out all unnecessary doublings. Our goal was to bring the band transcription as close as possible to what Beethoven intended in his original score.

The project took every moment of the director's spare time for two full weeks, but finally the job was done. He then asked me to "come and work the band" and arranged special evening rehearsals. I arrived the evening before my first rehearsal so we had time to talk, and so I had time to see the revised full score. I was very impressed with the effort. Working from the full score made the necessary changes obvious, and most of the correcting had already been done by the time I got there.

At my first rehearsal (after the first run-through), my host threw up his arms and exclaimed, "What a difference. That's it!" We now had the correct texture, clarity, and dynamics. Later at the State Festival the band was the rave of many and, of course, was rated "superior." Interestingly, one of the State judges wrote on the comment sheet, "I see you've done your homework."

Alterations to the Original Published Score for Festival Use

Check the rules of a Festival to make sure alterations of an original score are allowed. From a musical standpoint, this should be assumed, but it's better to be safe and check. Alterations of the original published score should be clearly noted on the score in ink. There are traditionally accepted practices of altering a score. These include:

- Doubling parts when appropriate

- Substituting instrumentation (when called-for instruments are missing)

- "Thinning" a score by removing redundant doubling

- Stylized alterations for concert performance of marches that are written full tutti

- Error corrections in the published score

• • •

Chapter 12: Proper Articulation

Don't Say "Tut", Say "Da"

Many players stop tones with their tongue using a "TUT" articulation. This is a very easy way to stop a tone, and it is a common bad habit. This "TUT" attack distorts the marcato style and actually slightly bends the pitch of each note. To correct these problems teach students to use "DAH" instead. All attacks should be "DAH", even heavy accents. The only way to make sure all players attack and release correctly is to check each player individually by hearing them play alone.

The release is a difficult concept to teach. The player must NOT use the tongue to stop the tone, instead teach them to concentrate on the "AH" part of the "DAH" syllable. This concept applies for wind players the majority of the time. However the reed players may use the tongue to stop the tone in some styles.

Brass Tongue Placement

Experience has shown me that many students use the wrong tongue placement for attacking notes. This assertion may seem extreme, but I found it to be true during the many years I taught at the University of Miami Band Camp. In Miami I taught students who came from all over Florida from many different bands and I found most of the brass players were articulating with incorrect tongue placement.

The most common problem I found was that flute and brass players allowed their tongues to touch their lips between their teeth instead of touching behind the top teeth. The correct placement finds the tongue touching behind the teeth as if producing a "TAH" or "DAH" syllable. It is incorrect to allow the tongue to touch the lips in a manner that would produce a "THU" syllable.

The only way to correct this problem is to hear and examine each student individually and pointing out what must be done to correct the problem. For students who have used the "THU" attack, changing to "DAH" is a discouraging process. "DAH" uses an entirely different embouchure muscle set, and the correct articulation may at first produce an immature beginner-like sound. This is because the new muscle set being used is weak, and it can only be developed by the player persistently articulating in the new, correct manner.

Students should be assured that the changeover will take only about three weeks if they are conscientious and stick to working on correcting the problem. They must be regularly warned not to slip back to the old tongue placement. If they do, it will only take longer to change to the correct tongue placement.

Woodwind Tongue Placement

Woodwind players have numerous articulation options to learn and develop. Depending on the length and size of their tongue they may prefer to anchor tongue (where the tip of the tongue is anchored behind the bottom teeth and the top of the tongue contacts the reed), or they may be more comfortable tonguing with the tip of the tongue. Either will work.

With reed instruments specific articulations are arrived at by varying the amount of tongue contacting the reed and by changing where the tongue actually touches the reed. Options range from barely touching the reed with the tip of the tongue to contacting the reed across the entire tip. Varying the air stream from strong to light also produces variations in articulation. Encourage your woodwind players to experiment and become proficient at all types of articulations at all dynamic levels.

• • •

PART 3:
TEACHING TECHNIQUES & SUGGESTIONS

Chapter 13: Rote Versus Fundamentals

"Let's start at the very beginning…"

--Maria (The Sound of Music)

Many band directors tend to teach too much by rote rather than from a firmly established foundation of strong musical fundamentals. Too little time is spent addressing basic music fundamentals. In rote-taught bands, playing skills are not advanced, the ability to read rhythms is poor, players don't know fingerings for all notes, players have little knowledge of musical terms, and they have little training in various styles of interpretation.

The tendency for some directors is to neglect the fundamentals and rush into preparing pieces for performance by simply teaching everything by rote usually with excessive repetition. Sometimes the end result is an acceptable performance, but the players usually play with little spontaneity. These directors tend to "hack through" the music measure-by-measure, detail-by-detail. In this type of situation, the band almost never develops sophistication. Students are spoon-fed basic musical elements, so much time is spent with repetition, and very little literature is covered; another factor that limits development.

Another secret to developing a mature band program is for the director to include training in basic musical skills and fundamentals in every rehearsal. It's like investing in a bank account, depositing a little every time the basic musical elements are taught. When a band has a strong background in the fundamentals, preparation of repertoire involves mostly interpretation in a minimum amount of time. There is no need for endless repetition and rote teaching. Well taught bands, properly grounded in the fundamentals, usually explore a lot of literature in a school year.

Fundamentals every player should know

1. Every student player should know the names of all the notes on their instrument including all flats, sharps, double flats, and double sharps for the entire range of the instrument.

2. Every student player should know the fingerings for all notes, including alternate fingerings, trill fingerings, and for trombonists, all primary and alternate slide positions.

3. All players should be able to recognize and identify all notes by name on the printed page.

4. All rhythm patterns should be understood, and players should be able to verbally count rhythm patterns using a "system" of counting. Students should know note values and duration combinations. These durations should be recognized in familiar rhythm patterns.

5. They should know all twelve major scales. This means knowing each scale by memory and with some degree of technical proficiency. Advanced students should be encouraged to learn all forms of the minor scales, as well as the diminished and augmented scales.

6. Teach the group solid fundamental sight-reading techniques and train them to follow the conductor. Sight-read every rehearsal and insist that they follow the baton. Create rubato exercises in order to enhance their ability to follow tempo and dynamic changes through conducting gestures and beat patterns.

7. Students should know basic articulation patterns and how they are executed in relation to different stylistic interpretations.

Routines

The most well taught players learn through well-established routines. The more extensive the routines are in a band program, the more sophisticated and mature the program will become. The term "routines" in this case refers to a highly developed program of training in fundamentals that addresses all areas of musicianship. Heading the list and most important are the fundamentals outlined above, but an outstanding band also operates using other well established routines. Other patterns to consider include: discipline, group behavior, attendance, punctuality, rehearsal procedure, equipment handling, and healthy attitudes and feelings ("esprit de corps").

Arrival at this high level doesn't just happen. At times the ensemble must be "preached to." In "sermons" students must be challenged from time to time with issues that deal with levels of expectation, discipline, moral values, personal responsibility, integrity, performance quality, etc. It's best to use one topic per "sermon" and only "preach once for a few moments during each rehearsal.

There is a difference between today's students and those of just a few years ago. It is good to read articles and books on this topic because writers on social issues will be able to shed light on the direction attitudes take today. Also, it should be mentioned that student attitude trends differ in different communities and schools of different socio-economic backgrounds. The successful band director must "tune in" on his particular situation and adjust accordingly.

Discipline

I have found that self-discipline is the most effective and successful way a band can reach the highest level. Demerits, penalty points, and detentions prove to be counterproductive and actually a waste of time. This doesn't mean that failure to measure is ignored. Grades can reflect behavior, but grades in band are a special consideration. They must reflect effort and participation, and everyone is expected to do his best and to participate in everything. So, almost everyone should be earning "A's. This becomes evident when we consider what a band would be like if a third of the students were "average" or below average.

Imposed discipline refers to a situation where the leader forces the group (usually through some form of threat) to conform. **Group discipline** develops when the individual members conform in order to avoid undue peer pressure. **Self-discipline** is the highest level and it depends on a highly developed set of moral standards in each individual. Strive to cultivate an environment where the students discipline themselves because they know what is right, and because of a sense of pride and commitment. Always expect everyone to function at the best of his or her ability and communicate that expectation.

Teaching Aesthetics

Some feel it is impossible to teach musical aesthetics. I disagree. In fact I think it is quite possible! In our bands we give students many opportunities to experience a high quality artistic activity. From these many experiences they learn to develop an aesthetic feeling for music. In other words, we first bring an aesthetic experience to the students (This way they come to know values, beauty, etc. all the elements we associate with the aesthetic). Then they begin to realize what it is to have an aesthetic experience.

Band directors have been known to say to their students, "Doesn't your musical sense tell you how to play that?" "How can you make that awful sound on your instrument?" or "Try to get a better sound on your instrument." In each case the student probably had not learned (or fully understood) correct musical concepts. An advanced musical sense hadn't yet been developed.

Students don't have any idea of what a good sound is on their instrument until they first produce a good sound. They must first hear a good sound, and then they must be led to experience what it takes to make a good sound. If players don't know what "good" is, they have no idea of how to achieve it.

Moral Values

A band director is in a unique position to be able to help students develop values more than most other teachers. Talk to the students about personal responsibility, being on time, being honest with one's self and others, and aspects of respect, character, and integrity. Brief discussions about these topics spread out over many months are much more effective than a long-winded sermon once a year. A band program that encourages high moral values will have a profound effect on the student members. A fine band experience can make a significant difference in changing the direction of a young person's life when the program encourages the correct values and high moral standards.

• • •

Chapter 14: "I Taught it, But Did They Really Learn It?"

Sometimes a band director makes an outstanding effort to teach some musical element(s) and, because he knows he was thorough and deliberate, he is satisfied that learning took place. I believe, however, that there are many times when directors do an excellent job presenting information, but ignore the more important task of following-up to see if their students actually learned what they taught.

A teacher may go through a fine delivery, assume that all students learned the material, and then go on to something else without checking to see if the band members actually learned anything. Never trust teaching something without following up to make sure the students actually learned. Following-up to see if each individual student learned is a critical part of training band students. The important thing to remember is that presenting information by saying it or showing it is only effective when the students actually understand, internalize, and are able to do whatever it is they are being taught. Make sure they learned it (see Duke, 2007).

Evaluating student learning can take many forms. Testing is one form of evaluation; playing tests, written tests, and verbal tests are options. However, too much testing can be a negative thing. I don't think anyone joined band to constantly be put to the test. Also, I've observed band directors wasting a lot of time testing the wrong things, or in the wrong way. However, sometimes testing is necessary. Some skills need careful evaluation and can take quite a bit of time to examine. Other skills can be evaluated quickly and easily. It all depends on what's being tested, how it's done, and how often.

Formative Assessment provides the information needed to adjust teaching and learning while they are happening. Formative assessment helps teachers determine next steps as learning progresses and can be thought of as part of the process of practice. Formative assessment is what normally occurs in rehearsals. Students play, directors assess and offer feedback, and students hopefully respond to the feedback!

Summative Assessments occur after instruction has taken place (sometimes weeks or months after) therefore they are tools to help evaluate the effectiveness of programs, but don't help in making short-term classroom adjustments (see Garrison & Ehringhaus, 2008). Summative assessments are like midterm or final exams or playing tests given after weeks or months of instruction.

Whatever you do, have a plan for using both types of assessments and use them wisely. Make sure they actually learned what you taught!

[AC: I found that giving playing tests to my beginning students on Thursdays/Fridays and again on Mondays was a very useful and motivating process. The end of week test provided a goal for the week, and the Monday test assured that many of the students practiced over the weekend. I also found that seating by test results was a motivator for the vast majority of the students. I always assigned a numerical grade to playing tests. This made seating easier (i.e. a 98 sat ahead of a 96) and also made calculating band grades much easier.]

• • •

Chapter 15: Ways to Develop a Better Ear

"Nonsense, the acoustics are getting better between your ears. The band sounds better because YOU can hear better."

--Richard W. Bowles

Some years ago I was talking to Richard W. Bowles, then Director of Bands at the University of Florida, about the recent improvements made to my band room by putting up more sound absorbing material. I told him, "The acoustics are getting better in the band room. We can hear so much better now. It's making a big difference in how good the band sounds." I will never forget his reply. He said, "Nonsense, the acoustics are getting better between your ears. The band sounds better because YOU can hear better."

The truth was, because of rehearsal room modifications the acoustics were a lot better, but he was right; the most significant factor was my improving "ear." The acoustics were getting better between my ears. I was acquiring what I now call "band director ears."

A band program can only be as good as the school facilities will allow. This involves many factors some of which are beyond the skill and control of the band director. Such things as poor rehearsal room acoustics, poor instrumentation, an inadequate budget, and limitations on the amount and quality of the equipment and uniforms are factors that limit the development of a band program. Probably the most significant factor that is beyond the control of the high school band director is the proficiency of the students that matriculate from the junior high or middle school. Competent instruction in the middle school feeder system is critical to the success of any high school band program.

On the other hand, there are some factors that are directly dependent on the ability and skill of a band director. Being able to perform well as an instrumentalist is no guarantee of becoming a successful band director. A high level of personal performance is proof of good basic musicianship, but many times outstanding players make poor band directors. The skills required of the successful band director include many things beyond individual performance capability. Good musicianship is certainly a prerequisite for dealing with advanced literature, but experience and hard work can improve personal musicianship significantly over time.

The Transformation

A band director has to go through a complete transformation from being a player to becoming a multi-faceted, highly skilled music teacher, conductor, and administrator who is keenly aware of the many factors involved in developing an outstanding program. This transformation hopefully will begin during the undergraduate years, but the big change usually comes with the first teaching job.

Hearing: The Most Important Skill

Of the many needed skills for being a successful band director, developing an analytical ear is probably the most important, yet it's the most elusive to acquire. Success at being able to develop outstanding performing bands depends more than anything else on developing "band director ears."

Our natural tendency is to hear selectively, to block out certain sounds and hear what we want to hear or what has our attention. We must overcome this tendency to hear subjectively and learn to hear objectively and analytically.

Some musical items are easier than others to find and correct. Wrong notes, rhythms, and basic dynamics are easy for most band directors to detect and correct. Most bands rarely play wrong notes or rhythms in festival performance. Items that appear in print on the score are usually well prepared. It's the elements that are not indicated on the score (such as sonority, blend, balance, intonation, and style) that are the more difficult factors to address. Mastery of these factors seems to depend largely on the director's ability to hear analytically. The band director who has developed his "band director ears" is the one who hears analytically, makes corrections, and consistently produces outstanding musical results.

Ways to Acquire "Band Director Ears"

1. Audio Record and Analyze Rehearsals

A good way to overcome the subjective ear and gain an objective ear is to record band rehearsals and later analyze the recordings. The microphone hears it like it is. Rehearsal recordings will tell the real truth where the ear alone will tend to be deceived.

Turn the recorder on before the students come in the door of the rehearsal room and record the entire rehearsal with no break. It's a good idea to be unobtrusive so the students ignore the fact they are being recorded. Bring the scores and a note pad home with the recording. While listening, make notes on the scores and note pad for reference for the next rehearsal. There will probably be many items needing attention and taking notes will be the only way to remember them all. Having the note pad and marked scores at the podium in later rehearsals greatly improves rehearsal efficiency.

Recording only once or twice is of little value; benefit comes from many repetitions of this process. Save and label recordings for future reference. It's important to have a good stereo system in the rehearsal room that includes a top-quality recorder and good microphones.

> The ear deceives, microphones don't.
> Microphones tell it like it really is.

This system of recording, playback, and score marking will also help identify errors in the rehearsal's extra-musical components. It may draw attention to excessive talking by the director, or possibly to a rehearsal pace that is too slow. The playback will quickly answer these questions and many others: Is the rehearsal dynamic and inspiring, or dull and boring? Does the director talk too much? Are students talking out-of-turn? Are background noises distracting? Are the director's instructions vague and wordy? Are the most important problems being worked, or is time being wasted on less significant items?

This process of repeatedly recording and analyzing your rehearsals helps one build a certain kind of ear. It's ear training for building "band director ears."

2. Bring in Outside Help

As discussed later in Chapter 16, "The Critical Confidant", invite a friend or colleague to rehearse your group. At some point in the rehearsal switch places. This allows the visiting colleague the opportunity to hear the band from the audience and to evaluate your techniques. After the rehearsal, sit down together and critique. Be willing to accept constructive criticism.

3. Attend Other Regional Festivals

If participation in band festivals is a part of your band's curriculum, then you should plan to attend and observe other regional band festivals on a regular basis. It's a good idea to do this as early as possible in the school year...at least two or three weeks before your local festival. This will allow you the opportunity to hear and evaluate performances by other groups and to compare them to where your group is at the time. Plan to do this every year. It offers a great perspective.

4. Purposely Alter Perspectives

Band directors have a problem when it comes to developing a good perspective. It's the nature of the job for a band director to see his program from too close a perspective. It's like looking at a mural from two feet away. It's easy to see the details but difficult to have perspective on the total scene.

It helps to get a fuller view by asking a colleague to conduct a rehearsal. This offers the band director the opportunity to see and hear from different positions and pick up on elements the visitor may bring out that were previously ignored or underprepared. It also offers the opportunity to get away from the podium and re-position eyes and ears. If possible, it's a good idea to have a special rehearsal in an auditorium so you can observe from the audience area while the colleague rehearses the band on stage.

Remember to bring a note pad and extra scores. The point of view afforded by listening from the audience will reveal many items needing attention that were previously overlooked. Taking notes will help you remember all of the many needed changes. It would also be a good idea to record these special rehearsals to capture comments from the guest conductor and later review his suggestions.

5. Rehearse in Another Environment

A good way to promote better hearing for your ensemble members and yourself is to rehearse a few times somewhere other than the band room. A different acoustical setting will allow everyone to hear the band differently.

Another good way to give everyone another perspective is to temporarily change the seating location of sections in the band for a few rehearsals. This allows the players to hear from another spot in the ensemble. It is also good to reseat within sections that have more than one part. For example, have students who normally play the 1st part move to the 3rd part for one rehearsal. It's not a good idea to change everybody at once. Moving one here and there, now and then is a very effective way to improve insight and awareness within the ensemble.

6. Listen to Live Performances

Seize opportunities to hear as many concert performances of other bands as possible. Concerts by neighboring schools, touring military bands, professional orchestras, and college and university ensembles are all good to attend. It is well worth the effort to hear numerous bands at contests and festivals. This may mean getting off the job for a day or more. Principals usually understand why a band director needs to be involved and will grant professional leave.

At band contests and festivals there are usually several other directors who are there to listen. Take advantage of this opportunity to exchange opinions and share evaluations. These valuable experiences are very important in developing a good perspective and ultimately to becoming an outstanding band director.

7. Listen to Recordings

Your musical standards are directly affected by what you regularly hear. Listening to "world-class" recordings on good stereo equipment helps you develop a more discerning ear and is an important contributing factor to becoming a successful rehearse and teacher. Listen to the pros. You need to know how it is supposed to sound!

8. Room Acoustics are Important

There are two factors to consider in room acoustics: reverberation and absorption.

Excessive reverberation may cause distortion. Distortion will make it more difficult for the players in the ensemble to hear each other. For example, if there are too many hard surfaces in the rehearsal room or if the walls are all parallel, a condition of rapid, very short echoes called "standing waves" may occur. This distortion makes it very difficult for players to hear critically. Avoid parallel reflective surfaces either by slanting walls or by placing absorbing surfaces (like drapes or acoustic tiles) opposite reflecting surfaces. Carpeting or other sound absorbing flooring helps a great deal.

The amount and the characteristic of sound absorbing acoustic material must be carefully considered. In the musical situation, the material used to absorb excessive sound volume must do so evenly across the audio spectrum. Most commonly used acoustic materials, such as those used in classroom ceilings, are designed to absorb room noise and are not appropriate for the musical environment. Most classroom and hallway noise occurs in the higher frequencies, so absorption materials are designed to absorb mostly in that range. Consequently they absorb almost nothing in the lower ranges (below middle C). If the wrong acoustic material is used in a rehearsal room, the ensemble may end up rehearsing in a room with much absorption at the high end of the spectrum and little absorption at the low end. The players will therefore be conditioned to overplay in the high range -- flutes, clarinets, oboes, and trumpets -- and to underplay in the bass ranges. In this setting the ensemble will learn the wrong balance. Then, when the group performs in a setting where the acoustics are normal, it will sound top-heavy with the upper instruments too loud and the bass instruments too soft. Unfortunately this unbalanced acoustic condition exists in many school rehearsal facilities.

Even when the band director knows an acoustical problem exists, sometimes school officials are reluctant to make the necessary changes. Administrators may question the credibility of the band director. They may not want to spend money on this seemingly technical problem only on the word of this one teacher.

Correcting poor acoustics depends on many factors. Some architects seem to have little understanding of music room requirements. Many new, visually beautiful facilities have been constructed over the years with terrible acoustics. It is difficult for officials to believe a band director's complaints are valid when an architect with credentials says everything is as it should be. Architects seem to want to make instrumental rehearsal rooms too "live." Seldom do we find a band rehearsal room that was designed too "dead."

Solving the Problem of Poor Acoustics

Since school officials rarely listen to acoustic recommendations from band directors, the director may need to engage an acoustical engineer as a consultant. This outside authority will lend credibility to the director's argument. School officials are much more likely to approve a special construction project to correct bad acoustics when they hear of the seriousness of a problem from an expert.

Hearing Musically is a Constant Challenge

Success from year to year depends on constantly cultivating and maintaining "band director ears." Don't expect to maintain keen hearing without some effort. It seems that critical hearing is like practicing on an instrument...Diligent practice is necessary to stay keen and perceptive. Musical maturity and insights will naturally develop from experience, but the ear is different. It must be constantly trained.

∙ ∙ ∙

Chapter 16: The Critical Confidant

The Nature of the Job

Problem #1: The school band director profession today is too demanding and complex for one person to master all aspects of the job.

Problem #2: The nature of the work routine tends to cause band directors to be isolated, "marooned", and unable to talk to colleagues or observe the work of others.

Problem #3: Working from the same spot on a podium in front of the same band day after day tends to lull the director into a very limited perception.

Problem #4: The artistic nature of the work -- band music, and particularly school students in performance -- involves many value judgments. Most issues in music are not "black or white", or "yes or no"; instead they are matters of discretion, taste, interpreting accepted styles, and common practice.

The Critical Confidant

It is almost impossible to be an outstanding band director today if one relies only on one's own resourcefulness. The scope of the required competencies of the job goes far beyond the abilities of one person. It's too much to expect one person to be an expert in all areas of running a band program. The solution: we must look for help from other band directors, from professional players, from master teachers of the instruments, from the music industry, and from the academic world. The challenge is to seek and find the best expertise. This means looking outside the school and outside the community. We must constantly be exposing ourselves and our students to the finest talents. We must learn to think "outside the box."

One very intense way to get help is to develop a close friendship with a colleague who will be able to offer constructive criticism...A CRITICAL CONFIDANT. This person must be trusted to keep all criticisms and dealings confidential, and they should command professional respect and be very competent in the areas of concern. The relationship must be such that criticism is readily accepted and there is a willingness to make suggested changes. The colleague should be someone who is noted for good judgment, a broad music education background, outstanding musical insights, and a proven track record.

Be aware that some outstanding band directors have trouble carrying on a dialog about how to improve bands. They have trouble verbalizing what they do, yet when put to task, they prove to be masters at bringing out the best performance qualities in their students through great musical and psychological insights. This type, like some performing artists, are masters of their craft but are limited when it comes to analyzing and explaining. Consider them teachers by example, or "coaches" rather than "teachers."

Make it common practice to invite your confidant to visit your group regularly. These visits should be well in advance of important concerts or evaluation festivals. It's good practice to do this not less than one month before a special event. Allow plenty of time to make changes and time for the changes to sink in. Guard against the tendency to wait until just before a performance to ask for help. A week or two before an event is too late. By then everything is set in the players' minds. It's best to bring in guest conductors and colleagues in the early stages of learning the music.

It's important for the host band director to closely observe the colleague at work. Do not sit in your office and do paperwork while your confidant rehearses! There should be a pre-arranged understanding that time will be set aside following the rehearsal to discuss items the colleague feels need attention.

Perspective

It's the nature of the job; band directors have difficulty maintaining an accurate perspective on their programs. The day-to-day pattern of work, being around the same students, and hearing the same sounds repeatedly seems to dull awareness of what needs attention. Problems are easily overlooked.

The day-to-day close-up working perspective is like looking at a painting from one inch away. A director must be able to draw back from the painting, to a position that will allow a true perspective.

The critical confidant may assist by offering suggestions from a more objective perspective, or he may have expert knowledge in a specific area. In either case, he will be a great help!

If at First You Don't Succeed...

As I said in Chapter 1, most prospective music teachers graduate with high ideals, intending to do an outstanding job. However, new teachers often stumble, make mistakes, and suffer bitter disappointments. Frustrations can come in many forms: irate parents, overbearing administrators, poor funding, difficulty in dealing with students, or the inability to get high festival ratings.

> The person who learns from their mistakes, learns from keen observation of fine examples, and learns to take constructive criticism will ultimately become a superb teacher.

After a period of not-so-hot teaching, a band director may reach a crucial moment when the bruised ego comes into play. The person may inwardly say either, "I better get busy and learn to do my job better", or "I did my best, and if that's not good enough, then that's too bad." This is a crucial point in a career. The best solution is (like the old song says) "pick yourself up, brush yourself off, and start all over again." The person who learns from their mistakes, learns from keen observation of fine examples, and learns to take constructive criticism will ultimately become a superb teacher.

• • •

Chapter 17: Host A Guest Conductor

"It's a guest! It's a guest! Sakes alive, well I'll be blessed!"

--Lumier (Beauty and the Beast)

Another technique that will help your program progress is to present concerts with well-known guest conductors/clinicians. 1) As I said before, band work is so demanding and complex that it's too much for one person to be expert in all aspects of the job. A guest clinician is usually able to offer some ideas that greatly help both the individual band director and the students. 2) As I mentioned in Chapter 16, working a school band program day-to-day requires dealing with many details from a close-in perspective. This inhibits a director's ability to draw back and see a true, overall view of the program and how it compares to other, similar situations. Someone from the outside usually has a more objective view and can offer suggestions for improvement, suggestions that address all aspects of the program, not just the musical elements. Therefore, a smart move the serious band director can make is to periodically bring in outstanding band directors, ask them to rehearse and perform with the band, and then accept their suggestions for improvement.

Each guest will have different strengths and will be able to offer unique insights and ideas. The outstanding musicianship and conducting skills of one guest may lead to valuable analysis and musical insights, while the "people skills" of another may point out new ways to deal with band personnel, parents, and administrators.

Some directors only invite guests for in-school rehearsals. This offers some benefits, but time limits the effectiveness of these sessions. The host should strive to provide extra rehearsals, cover the travel and accommodation arrangements for each guest, and find a way to offer financial remuneration for expenses as well as an honorarium.

Here is an effective plan for inviting a clinician/guest conductor. It involves more than a one-day visit:

Day One: Daytime:

- Guest travels to the session, checks into the hotel where the host has made reservations, and rests.

Day One: Evening:

- Host takes guest to an early dinner
- Evening special rehearsal (two hours)

Day Two: Daytime:

- Pre-arranged release of students from classes for special rehearsals; two hours in the morning and two hours in the afternoon.

Day Two: Evening:

- Concert performance featuring the guest conductor
- Definite plans for either an early or late dinner

Day Three: Morning:

- Guest travels home

If the guest's transportation is other than private auto, arrangements must include providing all transportation needs. Every situation is different and sometimes an administrator will not allow students to miss classes. If this is the case, the guest should arrive a day earlier and conduct special after school or evening rehearsals.

Most importantly, all details of the venture must be carefully planned. All parents, students, and administrators involved must be completely informed of all details. All financing must be accurately anticipated.

Hosting a guest conductor/clinician is a very powerful tool for broadening the students' experiences. When the guest conductor is a prominent figure in the band world, the event takes on added significance. When the final goal is a concert performance with a famous conductor, the students put forth their best effort. The resulting high-quality performance adds pride and distinction in a very special way.

• • •

Chapter 18: The Giant Metronome

I have learned that one of the most difficult musical elements for a band to master is perfect rhythm. I am not sure that "perfect" rhythm is possible, but excellent rhythm certainly is! Achieving an absolutely rock-solid, steady pulse is not easy. Listening to warm-up marches at contests and festivals is very revealing regarding the rhythmic control, or lack thereof, exhibited by many bands!

Some years ago one of the master Florida high school band directors was asked to do the All-State Symphonic Band. It's unusual to invite a high school director to conduct the top All State Band; this honor is usually reserved for a well-known college or military conductor. However, this gentleman had a reputation for having done exceptional work for many years, both with his own program and at one of the prestige summer music camps, so he was invited. I anticipated this All-State experience would be significant, so I decided I would observe every one of his rehearsals.

At his first rehearsal he didn't do a warm-up or any tuning. Instead he went right to the big number, the *Finale of Symphony #3* by Giannini. He began by asking the top snare drummer to play eighth notes at a loud dynamic level, and told him not to stop for any reason until told to do so. The pulse he generated was like a "giant metronome." He worked with the drummer for ten minutes until the pulse settled-in and was solid and steady.

Then he began to rehearse the piece. It immediately became clear to me why he took this approach. The players, even though they were the best in the state, rushed the short notes and drug the long notes. This master teacher and conductor was relentless...he stopped for nothing. They played almost all the way through the movement with the pulse vacillating, rushing and dragging. Then suddenly one of the more significant learning experiences in my career occurred. The band locked onto the pulse like a machine, and they continued to play with a very accurate and steady pulse. The irregular pulse problem had been solved!

Using the drummer as a giant metronome provided the same benefit to the ensemble as using a metronome provides an individual. This was the first time I realized a metronome could be used effectively with an entire band. The conductor rehearsed the entire band using a human metronome the same way an individual would use an electronic device in private practice. It was amazing to sit there listening to the pulse vacillate, then finally settle down and remain steady. The entire process didn't take more than twenty minutes. I later realized that this conductor knew the piece so well that he identified the problem before it occurred and went right to work establishing a steady pulse.

That incident was a revealing and dramatic moment in my learning how to solve a tenacious problem. Ironically, and sadly, this happened quite early in the morning, and there was not one other high school band director in that rehearsal to witness what happened.

Later that year, I was in the throes of preparing the Shostakovich *Festive Overture* for festival. Everything was going quite well, the difficult technical parts were mastered, the sonority was fine, but the band couldn't handle the offbeat patterns in the middle of the piece. They simply could not play those off-beats together at that fast cut-time tempo. Was this to be our "Achilles heel"? Then I remembered the giant metronome.

I got out my Dr. Beat electronic metronome, plugged it into the auxiliary input of the stereo system in the band room, and set it loud enough so the entire band could hear it while playing. I used an eighth note pattern. We rehearsed with this set-up for several rehearsals on both *Festive Overture* and the warm-up march. The giant metronome saved the day, and from then-on, whenever there was a problematic rhythmical passage in a piece, I used this technique. Often a band may seem to be holding a steady pulse, but when paced by the metronome, irregularities become evident. My advice is to use this technique on every extended rhythmic passage.

[Another reason for the off-beat problems in the Shostakovich is that the band arrangement commonly performed (Hunsberger) assigned the orchestra's double bass part to the bass clarinets! The large college symphonic band for which it was originally arranged had several bass clarinets – most modern bands only have one, and most orchestras have six to eight double basses. This scoring imbalance makes it difficult or impossible for all members of the ensemble to hear the downbeats. A good solution is to double the bass clarinet part with one or two tubas!]

• • •

Chapter 19: The Memorize & Look-Up Technique for Outstanding Performance

Student musicians are often taught the importance of closely watching their conductor, and this is a good thing. Tradition has the ensemble sitting in rows of arcs facing the podium with the music stands adjusted to allow the best angle to see the conductor. Conductors use a raised podium and the musicians are exhorted to "watch!" Still, most of the time, the students have their eyes on the sheet music and not on the conductor. We assume students are using their peripheral vision. We may be wrong!

For some reason, the need for constant eye contact to increase the quality of performance does not seem to be necessary for adult players. Even amateur adult musicians with limited playing skills seem to hear and see well. Peripheral vision may be more of a contributing factor for adult musicians and this would be an interesting topic to research. Anecdotal evidence would seem to suggest that adult musicians tend to perform better than younger musicians and the age of the musicians in major orchestras and other professional groups certainly seems to support this assertion. Some empirical research indicates that the determining factor is training (see Duke, Geringer, & Madsen, 1988; Fyk, 1987; Geringer and Witt, 1985). However, other studies have focused on the role of experience as well as practice as contributing factors to performance success (see Ericsson, Krampe, & Tesch-Römer, 1993). Whatever the case, age or experience, it appears safe to say that student musicians are not as adept as adults at watching both their music and their conductor. Conversely, adults, regardless of their level of playing ability, seem to be more aware of a conductor than students, even without direct eye contact.

After many years of working with both student and adult ensembles, I have learned that with younger players, regardless of their talent and level of musical achievement, direct eye contact with the conductor makes a great deal of difference; essentially, groups with students who watch the conductor perform better. When young players keep their eyes on the sheet music, they do not respond as well as when they have the music memorized and can keep their eyes on the conductor. Experience has shown me that there is a significant difference in the quality of the ensemble performance when young players have the music memorized so their eyes can remain focused on the conductor.

> Student musicians perform significantly better when all music is totally memorized allowing them to constantly watch the conductor.

For music directors who deal with school-age players, here is a technique that can greatly increase the quality of performance: Simply have the players memorize their music so they can look directly at the conductor during performance.

The Technique

This technique keeps the stands and music - it doesn't mean to avoid using sheet music. The setup is the same, with well-oriented stands, sheet music on the stands, and seating in arcs. This technique merely requires the players to keep their eyes on the conductor almost all of the time with only momentary glances down at the music.

When rehearsals begin on particular selections the players should be told they will be expected to play by memory by performance time. If told early enough, they will have no trouble memorizing. I have found that special rehearsal time devoted to memorizing is a waste of time. All that is necessary is for the conductor to reminded players repeatedly to look up as much as possible so that by performance time everything will be memorized. Precision, attentive listening, good balance, intonation, and tone will all improve when the students begin to focus their attention away from the printed page.

Look Up For Entrances

A very effective device that should be part of a band's "routine" is to have all players get into the habit of looking right at the baton for all entrances, not looking down at the music. The players should "memorize" the first measure all entrances, look at the conductor while playing each entrance, and then look down at the music after the first measure if necessary. This makes for precise and definite entrances, and it signals the conductor that the players are alert and engaged.

• • •

PART 4:
MUSIC & MUSIC PREPARATION

Chapter 20: Method Books

How to Use Beginning Method Books

Be relentless in your thoroughness! Start at the beginning of the book. Cover every detail on every page. **Never** skip-over sections or pages found in the method book. Be extremely meticulous and your students will benefit from a music education well grounded in strong fundamentals. You will benefit personally because your program will constantly improve. Supplement the book with sessions on proper tone production as outlined elsewhere in this book. Exceptional beginning band instruction is the secret to all great band programs! Be relentless in your application of fundamentals.

What to Do When the Method Book Gets Dull

In beginning band classes, students sometimes get mired down and stop making progress. They get bored and discouraged, and all momentum seems to stop. It's important to solve this problem as soon as it is suspect. Students at this stage sometimes experience a change of attitude and may elect to drop out. This sort of attitude is contagious and, if left unresolved, can lead to several potentially outstanding students leaving the program. Not good.

I found when I used only one method book there would be times when the students got bored. During these lulls progress became difficult. I found by merely introducing a "new" book, which was actually just another method book at the same level, the interest returned and the kids became enthusiastic again. I was amused to note they maintained interest and progressed while covering exactly the same issues and problems that seemed uninteresting in the first book. All it took was a "new" book, a few new tunes, a different look, and away they went.

I found it more practical to have each beginner purchase his own copy of the main method book and have the band furnish a set of supplemental books. That way I could use them for a short period, collect them, and then issue them again at a later time. This trick of presenting the same material in a new and different package is sometimes all it takes to regenerate interest. The important factor is that this trick can keep students from quitting during those shaky beginning months.

More Flexible Conductor Method Book Manuals

This is an idea that allows lesson plans and even custom written supplementary materials to be integrated into your method book manuals.

Most school systems have fine facilities for laminating. Classroom teachers often laminate many of their materials in order to preserve them. The band director also can take advantage of this service to preserve materials that are used repeatedly.

Take apart the manual and laminate each page. Punch holes in the laminated pages and insert the pages into a three ring binder in the order they were before. It's now possible to insert lesson plans and supplementary scores in order in the manual. Plus, the plastic protection on each sheet will make the manual last longer when used year after year.

Beyond the Method Books

The use of well-written method books in training school wind instrument players has had an important influence on effectively teaching students in large ensemble classes. It's impossible for any book to cover everything; some aspects of training must come from the teacher. Some items, such as learning a new note or learning how to play a familiar tune are effectively covered in most method book series. Other factors in student training tend to be left out and must receive special attention.

Almost all wind students receive their instruction from the beginning stages through intermediate from these method books. Much of the success of the band movement can be attributed to efforts of the authors/composers of these popular series. The books are written in a progressive way. They go from easy to hard, simple to complex. The authors carefully design these methods to present material one step at a time.

These band "text books" have helped to relieve some of the burden of lesson planning for the director. The orderly presentation of material, sometimes there are suggestions on how to teach it, is published in method books. Effective as method books are, instruction must go beyond what these series offer if it is to be complete. Certain areas need special consideration.

A System of Counting

Some method books include a system of counting rhythms; others do not. Verbalizing, saying the rhythms out loud by identifying the beats by the number, all forms of subdivisions, and all rest values is a skill each student must have. It becomes the responsibility of the teacher to add this required instruction. Its inclusion should be a daily event in the beginning band setting.

Sonority Training

I will say it again; one of the most important factors in the proper training and development of the wind instrument student is learning to be able to achieve good sonority when performing in an ensemble. Without this ability, the individual and the entire ensemble will never be able to achieve better than mediocre results. Intonation and tone quality will always suffer until sonority is thoroughly taught.

It's difficult to write music and text materials into method books that deal with sonority training. The teacher must 1) have a good concept of how and what to teach for students to be able to play in tune with a good tone quality and 2) how to include this instruction in each day's rehearsal. Existing materials must be adapted. Sections in the method books and appropriate sections from compositions and chorales are the usual sources.

Embouchure Training

The teacher must be able to instruct students on the proper development of their embouchure and correct placement of the tongue for proper articulation and response. Left on their own, students can develop serious bad embouchure habits that will make superior playing impossible. Usually nothing more than a picture and a few comments are mentioned in the method books. [See chapter 4, *Proper Embouchure Focus*]

Establishing Practice Habits

Some method books contain blank practice schedules with spaces to be filled in by parents confirming home practice. From the first beginning stages, the teacher must establish the idea that playing an instrument demands regular practice. The requirement of a certain number of minutes a week and a system of regularly checking on each student may be used in a beginning wind instrument program. Once the habits and expectations are established in the beginning band, students will continue this pattern well into senior high school and beyond without the need for practice sheets.

As I mentioned earlier, regular playing tests and seating based on the results will do much to encourage practice and develop healthy practice habits. I like this approach better than practice sheets because, in most students, it fosters a desire to perform well when tested and a desire to move up in their section.

• • •

Chapter 21: Marking Music

Marking the score and parts before a selection is passed out can save a lot of time and help eliminate rehearsal distractions. Some numbers have very poor rehearsal letters or interpretive markings. More rehearsal letters/numbers as well as markings emphasizing certain dynamics, articulations, etc., will help improve efficiency when rehearsing a new piece.

Obviously, certain selections are more important than others in a program. They may be more difficult to prepare or they may be intended for some special event such as an important concert or a contest or festival. Spending time marking the music in these selections can make a big difference in the quality of the final performance.

Before handing out a piece, take the time to study the score well enough to find potentially troublesome spots. Once the score is thoroughly examined and marked, you can mark anticipated trouble spots on each of the individual parts before they are handed out. Using a colored pencil or highlighter will make your markings easier for the students to see.

Markings to Consider

1. Some older publications had NO rehearsal letters; some newer ones have too few. In either case, adding more rehearsal letters or numbers will speed up rehearsal efficiency.

2. Numbered measures are more expedient than letters. Saying "start at 45" is quicker than having to say, "Start five measures after letter G", thus causing all of the players to have to count five bars.

3. Sometimes other markings can be used as a "rehearsal letter." Just as the *D.S. sign* can be used as a rehearsal letter, so can other marks if every player has the same mark in the same location.

4. Everyone who has worked professionally is familiar with the hand drawn caricature of a pair of "glasses" which is often used to draw attention to a potential problem in the music. Teach the students to use this little cartoon- it works!

5. Just circling something with a pencil is usually all the warning that is needed.

6. Numbering every measure on the score and all individual parts makes it possible to more efficiently rehearse a selection. This job is too time consuming for the band director to do alone; the players should be asked to number their own parts. To assure accuracy, it's a good idea to provide the students with checkpoints along the way. First number each measure of the score and double check for mistakes. Then make a list of where important checkpoints are in the music. Such a list might look like this:

NOBLE MEN - by Henry Fillmore

- 5 - First strain
- 22 - Second strain
- 39 - Trio
- 55 - Repeat sign in trio (break strain)
- 71 - Double bar in trio (last strain)
- 87 - Last measure

Have all players notate just the check-point measures during rehearsal and ask them to finish numbering every measure outside of rehearsal time. Follow-up to make sure they did it!

• • •

Chapter 22: Folio Management

Miscellaneous Parts

Label Folio #1 "Conductor."

Label folio #2 and #3 "Miscellaneous Parts", then continue with the regular order after that. This way all of the extra parts are right there with of the rest of the issued music. Avoiding having to run back to the library every time someone needs a part saves time.

Labeling Folios

In large sections, like the clarinets, next to the folio number show the part plus the place in the section:

1 Bb Clarinet - A

1 Bb Clarinet - B

2 Bb Clarinet - A

2 Bb Clarinet - B

3 Bb Clarinet - A

3 Bb Clarinet - B

Two Sets of Folios

If you do a lot of sight reading (and you should), your librarians will have a problem trying to keep up with the demands of passing out and collecting the sight reading music. They usually need a lot of time to work on a folio set in a place where no one else has access. This way they can do an orderly job of sorting the sheet music without interruptions.

Use **two** sets of folios at all times labeled "SET A" and "SET B." Either set can be taken out of circulation for several days until the work of sorting the sheet music is done. Before each concert; put just the program music in one folio set, and everything else in the other set. This way only the needed music is carried to the concert stage.

Performance Folios

To avoid the disaster of a mix-up in music, after the last rehearsal, and well before the performance, collect and check every folio yourself to make sure everything is in order. Pack all the folios, baton, tuner, etc. together in a special well marked music case. The band director should trust no one but himself in preparing the folios for the performance. Remember; keep all non-performance music in the other folio set.

Make packing the music case a "ritual" before loading out for a performance to be sure nothing is left behind. It is safer to "put all the eggs in one basket" and not trust the students in the preparation of the performance sheet music.

Catalog Each Sheet of Music

Have the librarians stamp the library catalog file number on the back of every piece of sheet music. For example, C-132 would be selection 132 in the concert music set. When stray music is found long after a piece has been filed away, the stray can be immediately returned to the right file without having to look it up. This is particularly helpful with marching band music.

The Jazz Band "Book"

Keep the jazz band folios set up like the road bands did in the big band era. Collect and maintain many tunes in the "book" in numerical order. Then call up the tunes by number. You have to constantly remind the students to keep the book neat and in order. It's easy to keep as many as 80 jazz band tunes in a regular concert band size folio.

Sheet Music

Idea #1: To save time in dealing with sheet music in circulation, it's a good idea to keep the folders/boxes apart from the main library in a file cabinet in the main rehearsal room near the podium. Keep a box in the top drawer of the file cabinet for lost and found parts.

Idea #2: Campaign to get students to purchase their own method books, etude collections, solos, and ensembles. In areas where there are no sheet music dealers the band director will have to obtain materials for students.

• • •

Chapter 23: Preparation and Performance of Marches

[Harold B. Bachman, Director of Bands Emeritus, University of Florida, presented a clinic/lecture in February of 1965 entitled "Styling of Standard Marches." Earlier in his career Bachman had been director of "Bachman's Million Dollar Band", one of the last of the professional concert bands. I contacted Reid Poole, who followed Bachman as band director and later became Head of the Music Department at U. of F., in the hope that he had a copy of Bachman's lecture. He did, and it is from these notes that much of the following is presented.]

Sometimes directors don't give enough careful attention to the preparation and interpretation of marches. The following are ideas to consider when dealing with marches. Just because a march is a recent publication doesn't make it better. Many of the old lyre-size marches are among the best ever written. The present time, unfortunately, is not the "golden age" of marches.

Many of the best marches are published in street or music lyre size and are scored "full tutti." This was done so the music could be used by any size group from a small circus band or a military band on parade, to a large symphonic band in concert. While the tutti sound may be preferable in some instances, it's possible to add tonal variety (such as changing voicing or moving the emphasis from one voice to another) when playing the marches in a concert setting.

The professional concert bands of Sousa, Fillmore, Karl King, Bachman, etc., did not play marches "full tutti" all the way through. The composers almost always stylized the marches.

A recent trend by some arrangers is to slightly alter a march that's in public domain and publish it in full size concert format. Usually the full tutti format has been untouched. This is confusing to the purchaser who purchased a recently published concert size version of a famous march with "arranged by" or "adapted by" under the name of the composer. However, the music is basically the way the composer wrote it -- full tutti. So, even though the piece is printed in a new format, it is still pretty much the same as it was in the original quick-step size. It will still need to be stylized if the conductor wishes to use authentic performance practices.

It is wise to evaluate the older compositions carefully. When compositions only include a limited score, it's a good idea to look at every part individually to get the total picture. There is nothing wrong with doing a little rewriting or marking parts if it's done in good taste, and done to make a piece more playable.

Keep in mind many of the march composers never wrote a score first – they wrote from memory. Karl King and Henry Fillmore were both known for this. In 1953 while visiting Henry Fillmore at his home, I remember seeing the parts of the "North-South College All Star March" on his desk in various stages of completion. I never saw a full score, just the parts. When I asked about the score, Henry said, "Oh, that's the last thing I do for the publisher." Fillmore said, "I write the first cornet part, then the first trombone part, then the bass part, then fill in all the rest." Years later I realized something amazing about his house. He didn't have a piano!

The Medium

Consider the original medium for which the march was intended...such as street parade, circus, school song, or strictly concert performance. This doesn't mean it must be used for that only. As I said earlier, the tradition of writing "full tutti" marches allows latitude for adaptation and stylization.

For example, I don't suggest using Fillmore's "Rolling Thunder" for a street parade; however his "Men of Ohio" and "Orange Bowl" were written for parade use, although today they are often used in concert performance. Many marches work in several settings.

Grading

For school use we need to consider grade level. Easy and medium-easy would obviously be used in junior high or middle school bands. It pays to examine the difficulty of particularly the inner parts when considering marches for younger groups.

Compositional Structure

Consider the compositional structure. For example, Sousa emphasized harmonic rhythm and was not much on florid woodwind figuration and counter melodies. Fillmore, on the other hand, was big on writing fancy woodwind figurations and counter melodies, particularly in his more difficult marches.

With certain composers, much of the time the trombones, baritones, and tenor saxophones are in unison, usually on a counter melody.

Many marches are voiced like "Dixieland" music. The first trumpet plays the melody, the clarinet plays the harmony note above, the trombone is on the counter melody, and the tuba has the bass part.

Although discussed later, the tradition of furnishing a limited score should be mentioned now. In earlier days the "score" was simply the solo cornet part with additional cue notes. In later years publishers began to furnish a two line score. Both of these are only sketches and omit much detail. In today's educational setting, if a band director intends to thoroughly prepare a march, the limited score won't do. He must take it upon himself to prepare his own full score before the music is passed out.

Earlier composers wrote only a Db piccolo part. Modern piccolo players play C piccolos, so these older parts must be either transposed at sight or rewritten. Some writers wrote quite high for the clarinet making the parts hard to play in tune. At the same time, parts for other instruments may be much easier. Older numbers often include only one alto sax part. This can create balance problems when there are several alto saxophones in a band.

There are several ways of writing for cornets. When there are special trumpet parts I don't suggest giving these parts to the weakest players at the bottom of the section. Rather, assign the trumpet parts to players near the top of the section next to the solo or first cornet part. These parts are important.

Earlier marches often include only Eb horn parts. Either have the players transpose Eb parts or write out special F Horn parts.

Earlier 3rd trombone parts were simply the tuba part 8va. If you have good tuba players you can eliminate the 3rd trombone part when it's a duplicate of the bass part and use only the 1st and 2nd trombone parts.

Sometimes only one baritone part, either treble or bass, is provided. It's up to the player to be able to read both clefs, otherwise write out the needed part. (Insist that they learn to read bass clef!)

In older publications, some parts indicate a D.S. but other parts are fully written out. This can create confusion in rehearsal, if not noticed and explained early on.

Styling of Standard Marches for Concert Performance

I recommend never playing marches full tutti all the way through. Style them by altering certain parts. If at all possible listen to recordings of Sousa's band or consult reference books and articles on Sousa, Fillmore, King, etc., Both Sousa and Fillmore styled their marches a certain way and then played them that way again and again.

If you are unable to obtain information on authentic performance practices here are some ideas:

Leave out an entire section of instruments for one strain and then reintroduce them later. Or have a section play a strain 8vb (down an octave) while leaving another section out. There are many possibilities.

Here is a commonly used format:

- Introduction and 1st strain - as is
- 2nd strain, first time - trumpets lay out the 1st time, with the rest of the band playing softer
- 2nd strain, second time - full tutti and a fuller dynamic from all
- Trio, 1st time - drums, trumpets, oboe, and flutes lay out, maybe clarinets 8vb
- Break strain - full tutti

- Trio last time - full tutti with emphasis on certain accents and/or counter melody

Here is a brief note from Henry Fillmore to Harold Bachman, then Director of Bands at the University of Florida, detailing how he would like the march Gifted Leadership prepared for a performance he was going to conduct at the University of Florida in 1955. This letter was still in the folio with the music in the **University of Florida band library the last time I was there!**

"Dear Harold:

Gifted Leadership --

- *Intro -- as is--*
- *1st strain -- as is -- with good accents on 2nd beat in 1st and 3rd measures*
- *Same on 9th and 11th*
- *2nd strain -- as is -*
- *Trio -- 1st strain, drums tacet. Interlude -- everybody in*
- *Last strain, 1st time -- drums out -- basses mf -- woodwinds good and strong*
- *On repeat -- everybody going to town -- bass drum watch for accents*

That's it --

As always,

Henry"

Some Styling Ideas by Section

At least one flute player should play piccolo, but piccolo should not be used all the time. In the suggested format above, the piccolo would tacet with the trumpets.

Flutes can tacet a strain, drop an octave with the other upper woodwinds, or be featured by themselves on obbligato lines.

Sometimes the clarinet parts can be altered for one strain by dropping them an octave and/or by having all in the section play off the 1st part so everyone is playing the melody in the lower octave.

In Fillmore marches the upper woodwind obbligato lines are often featured by having them play louder than the rest of the band for one strain.

Saxes and clarinets can be featured by raising their dynamics and cutting out some brass (probably the trumpets). This is usually done the first time through a repeated strain.

Cornets are usually dropped so other sections can be featured. When there are separate trumpet parts, the cornets can tacet leaving just the trumpet figuration played.

Sometimes, when the cornets drop out, the horn off-beat harmonic rhythm is dropped too. This is usually done when the clarinets drop to the low register and join the baritones and saxes on the melody. This scoring features only the bass line and the melody and block harmony.

The trombones can tacet along with the cornets. Another idea is to bring out the counter melody line by raising the dynamics of the trombones in unison with the baritones and tenor sax.

The percussion is often omitted (or subdued) for one strain. Special accents are where the percussion really shines. Fillmore marches are famous for these moments.

Bachman points out, "Bass Drum and Cymbals are to be played together unless otherwise indicated...solos will be indicated for one or the other as needed." He indicates places where there will be "these special little accents (where) I like to have more 'zing' than 'boom'."

Make sure snare drummers are playing rudimentally correct with exactly the right number of strokes in each rudiment or figuration. Some may be using a 5 stroke roll while others use a 7 stroke roll. One player may use a flam and another use a ruff. This makes for a lack of precision.

The bass drum muffling should be determined by what the bass drum accompanies. The bass drum should be large and tuned low. Use no muffling so when desired it can be played with lots of 'ring.' Try this: Hand or knee muffle the softer strains, then take off all muffling and let it 'boom' or 'ring' for the "special little accents." Let it ring during the full tutti strains along with what Fillmore called "more 'ching' from the cymbals."

Ideas on Rehearsing Standard Marches

Number All Measures

Many marches have no rehearsal letters, so it's a good idea to have the students number every measure. Check older publications. Some of them may contain parts with repeated sections while others contain written out repeats.

Mark Parts

Before passing out the parts, mark each part to indicate special accents, voicings, tacets, etc. (This seems like a lot of work, but it saves much rehearsal time in the end.) After numbering the score, put a list like this on the board for everyone to copy:

Gloria by F. H. Losey, arranged by Julius S. Seredy

Section	Measure number
1st strain:	9
2nd strain: Trio:	42
break strain:	62
last strain:	79
last measure:	95

Make a Full Score

For important performances, it's worth the time and effort it takes to make your own full score. It's foolish to try to work from the limited two or three line condensed score when preparing for a serious performance. A full score makes more precise rehearsing possible. With a full score each part can be checked for accuracy.

Rehearsal Techniques

Early in the preparation of a march rehearse at a very slow tempo without percussion. This allows all players to hear every inner rhythm and all secondary parts.

Check each player's concept of the marcato style. Check articulation by making sure all releases are uniform and the space between notes in the marcato march style is uniform throughout the band.

It is important "to take a march apart" in rehearsal by working some of the lines individually. For example, have just the tubas and horns play together, or have just the high woodwind obbligato play, or have just the melody and underlying matching harmonic rhythm play (e.g. 1st, 2nd, and 3rd cornets plus alto saxes).

Use the "Giant Metronome" Technique

At various stages of preparing any composition with a lot of rhythmic complexity I suggest using the amplified metronome discussed in chapter 18. Just as a metronome benefits an individual, it can be amplified and used to benefit an entire band. You can amplify it through the band room stereo system or a guitar or keyboard amplifier. You may find that the ensemble's pulse is more unstable than you suspected!

When students have a problem playing off-beats accurately, set the "giant metronome" for subdivisions of the beat and rehearse the music at various tempos.

Rehearse the ensemble at various different tempos up until the last few rehearsals. Then use the exact performance tempo.

Recommended CD Recordings

- Allen, E. W. Sounds of John Philip Sousa -- Authentic Rehearsal Techniques for the Preparation and *Interpretation of Recorded Marches*. The United States Army Band. This CD and an extensive booklet were available from the American School Band Directors Association (ASBDA). Membership in ASBDA was not required for purchase.

- Bourgeois, J. (1980). Semper Fidelis: Music of John Philip Sousa [CD], Washington D.C. United States Marine Corps. [This C D and others are free for the asking available only to institutions. An informative booklet is included. Your school band is an institution, so I suggest your request letter be on band stationery. Write to the Marine Band at the Marine Barracks, Washington, D.C. and ask for their latest offerings including this one. Also ask to be put on their mailing list.]

- Clark, N. A., Miller, W.C. (1999). *Military Escort: The Music of Henry Fillmore*. Warner Robins, GA: The Band of the United States Air Force Reserve. [Now available through Amazon]

- Reynolds, H. R. (1993). ON PARADE--World's Greatest Marches. University of Michigan Symphonic Band. Quintessence CDQ2016. [You may find this one in the discount rack. I paid $4.99 for it.]

Other References

- Bachman, H. B. (1965). Styling of Standard Marches (Lecture). University of Florida.

• • •

PART 5:
FESTIVAL PREPARATION IDEAS

Chapter 24: Festivals and Contests

With the emphasis in education today [1997] on validity and accountability, the Band Evaluation Festival movement stands tall. It's a valuable "tool" for motivating and encouraging high standards and I offers the opportunity for critical evaluations from respected colleagues. There is much confusion today on the terminology used for evaluation events. In earlier years, all band evaluations were called contests. This was probably a holdover from the pre-world war II days when there were national band contests that truly were competitions to see which band was the best in the nation. Evaluations where only ratings are given are not contests. In recent years the term "festival" has been used to better describe evaluation events. Unfortunately, the term "contest: has often been used for band festivals where judges give quality grades and no winners are chosen. There is absolutely no competition among bands at festivals.

Evaluation festivals often use three judges. This is done to help avoid ties in the grading and also to offer three different opinions. The final rating is an average of the scores from all three ratings. With more than one judge involved the results are more apt to be accurate.

A "Festival" grading system may look like this:

Score	Name	What it Really Means
I	Superior	The highest possible rating
II	Excellent	Still a good performance
III	Good	Actually below average
IV	Average	Very weak
V	Poor	Very, very weak (Have you ever considered selling shoes?)

The reputation of a band director and his band is often largely determined by the results of festival ratings. Now that's accountability! The most successful directors are noted for producing bands that are consistently judged "Superior" at State Festival year after year.

The Road to a Superior at State Festival: A Summary

This is a matter of opinion, but I would recommend the following plan:

Don't think that working just the festival music for weeks on end to the exclusion of other material is the way to a superior rating. In fact, this approach is detrimental to the students and will actually inhibit their development. The road to an outstanding band, one that is consistently rated "superior" is complex, but some of the way down that road is quite clear.

There are two basic requirements to developing a superior program:

1. There must be enough promising players to complete the instrumentation

2. The instrumentation must be a fairly well balanced

Be careful to avoid too many treble and not enough bass instruments. There is virtually no hope of superior results with imbalanced instrumentation. It is up to the persuasive abilities of the band director to get players to switch to one of the needed instruments. Students are reluctant to give up their first instrument for fear they will not do well on the second. One way to relieve this anxiety is to ask them to "just try it" and to "double" on the new instrument. If they learn to double they will be considered a player of **two** instruments. This approach usually works. When the players find that they do well on their new instruments, they won't think of switching back.

One of the Biggest Mistakes

One of the biggest mistakes made by many band directors is teaching by rote rather than by building a strong fundamental foundation in each player. "Rote teachers" usually work exclusively from the printed music. They rote teach every rhythm, dynamic, note, and fingering. These directors work measure by measure, stopping frequently, and talking excessively because everything has to be explained. They answer "how does it go?" by singing the part to the students – this is the essence of rote teaching!

Technique is usually poor in a band with weak fundamentals, so the director relies on excessive repetition to "pound in" the technique, and so the students will remember what has been rote learned. This approach is very limiting. Much time is required to make meager advances. The process is boring to the players and stressful for the band director.

Fundamentals-based band directors are usually known for making superior ratings year after year. Their approach is much different. Their emphasis is on developing in all players a strong foundation of proper musical fundamentals and proper playing habits. When it is time to work on festival literature, the players are so well developed they seem to play the music with ease. The superior director pays little attention to the details on the written parts. The players accurately execute everything on the printed page. Most of the rehearsal time is devoted to style and interpretation – to the music!

In a band where all players are thoroughly trained in the fundamentals, there is less need for frequent stops in rehearsals. The group will only stop to touch up spots or to come to an agreement on some interpretive question. The ensemble develops "musical momentum."

Bands in well-developed programs, regardless of their concert schedule, spend time reading much literature that may never be programmed. The players approach reading new literature with ease and confidence, and they enjoy the process. Reading is fun. Playing well is fun. Band is fun!

The Fundamentals

Start very early to develop a broad foundation in the musical fundamentals. Strive to develop in each student a thorough knowledge in these areas:

1. The ability to play with a characteristic professional tone.

2. An understanding of intonation problems and the ability to play well in tune.

3. The fingerings/positions/valve combinations of all notes on the instrument, including alternate fingerings/positions/valve combinations.

4. Recognition and execution of basic rhythm patterns.

5. A system of counting (like the "Eastman System"). Be able to verbally count all rhythm patterns

6. The names and locations of all notes on the music staff. M

7. Musical terms and their meanings

8. Dynamics, their characteristics, and tendencies

9. The various styles and their basic interpretations

10. Familiarity with articulations

11. Phrasing, shaping, and contouring musical phrases

12. Understanding and following conducting gestures and cues

Music Selection

Select and distribute performance music as early in the school year as possible. This should be a very calculated and careful process. Consider the strengths and weaknesses of the band. Different pieces have reputations for being suitable in different ways for festival evaluation. Look for the recommendations and opinions of prominent colleagues. There may be a "preferred music list" to choose from. One of my colleagues once said, "Half the battle is selecting the right music." Ask for help if you need it!

Pre-marking parts can save much time before they are passed out. As soon as the music is in the folio, have all players number the measures. Outline the pieces by measure number on the board. [This process is discussed in more detail near the end of Chapter 21].

Get to know the music early, but rehearse it only occasionally at first. It is important not to focus on just these few numbers. As festival time approaches, plan the rehearsals so that preparation peaks about two weeks before the performance. Be absolutely sure about the thoroughness of the preparation – yours and the band's.

Early to midway through the preparation time seek the advice, help, and opinions of respected colleagues. Bring in these outstanding band directors to "work the band." One of the biggest mistakes made is to wait until it is too late to bring someone in. Asking someone to come in a week before festival is a waste of time. All the person can do at that point is say, "Good luck!" By then it's too late to make changes. The time to bring someone in is at least a month before the event.

A good saying to remember: "If you go to festival hoping to get a "superior", you'll get an "excellent." If you go to festival knowing you'll get a "superior", you'll get a "superior." Remember, your expectation level, and your vision, are in control now. Your band will operate at your highest level of expectation. It starts at the top (see Deming, 1986).

Also remember; don't make the mistake of working only marching band music during the early part of the school year. The fundamentals and the concert band setting must be worked from the first days of school. Waiting until the end of marching season is too late!

The value of the evaluation, being judged by one's peers, depends entirely on how the band director uses the activity. It can be a very strong motivator to bring the bandsmen to the peak of their abilities. It can be a guiding way to help make plans for the future. One thing is for sure; taking a band to festival puts the band director's "feet to the fire." It exposes for all to see and hear. It establishes in everyone's mind the standards in the band movement, and it gives a band director a way of evaluating his work.

The Sound

Directors sometimes make the mistake of not exposing students to "the professional sound." It is your job to make sure they have superb sounds to model. Equip the rehearsal hall with a quality stereo system. Regularly take a few minutes from rehearsal to listen to "definitive" recordings. In a sense, the stereo system may be the most valuable "instrument" in a band program. With *You-Tube* and the many other online sources available, it is easy to find examples of professional quality wind band, jazz, and orchestra performances.

The most impressive way to teach students "a great sound" is to arrange for them to hear great live performances. Announcing a concert and expecting many students to attend is not going to work; only a few will attend. The answer is to make it a required event. Provide school busses and take the entire band. There are usually colleges and universities in the area, and military bands make regular concert tour appearances. Having the entire band attend a concert is a powerful tool in developing the correct concepts and mind-set in students. The rewards are well worth the effort it takes to arrange such trips. Students need to hear their band director say things like; "Now this is what you should sound like" and "Did you notice how professionally they acted?"

Too many times over the years when I asked students I was judging if they had ever attended a concert by an outstanding band, they answered "no." The bottom line: The student players must first have a concept of what they should sound like and how they should perform before they can be expected to achieve their goals. You must provide examples of that concept.

Recommended Reading

- Lussy, M. (1892, 1952). *Musical expression: accents, nuances, and tempo, in vocal and instrumental music* (Vol. 25). Novello, Ewer and co. H. W. Gray Co. agents for USA

- VanderCook, H. A. (1942). *Expression in music.* Rubank. (Revised and published by Rubank in 1952)

- Voxman, H., & Gower, W. (1954). *Rubank advanced method, saxophone: an outlined course of study designed to follow up any of the various elementary and intermediate methods.* Chicago: Rubank.

• • •

Chapter 25: Countdown To a Superior

For Solo and Ensemble Festival

This is a step-by-step guide to the selection, preparation, and performance of solos and ensembles for contests and festivals. Most adjudication of solos and ensembles is in conjunction with either district or state band festivals that usually come in the middle of the second semester. This timetable is designed with that time frame in mind, however it may be altered to meet the needs of any particular calendar. Make sure each individual participating in the contest or festival has a personal copy of this chapter. (Feel free to reproduce it as needed).

Preparation for Solo and Ensemble Festival

Disappointing ratings are often the result of either poor planning, or of being unaware of certain requirements of a particular contest or festival. Everyone participating, both the directors and the students, should be familiar with festival rules. There is almost always a rulebook or a printed guide for each festival and this source should be carefully reviewed well in advance of any preparation. Scheduling is also always a concern, and finding and coordinating with accompanists can be a challenge. Blank adjudicators' forms are usually supplied in festival/contest rulebooks. If not, ask for a copy. Each participant should have a copy of the adjudication form in order to better understand what areas the judge will be evaluating.

Students: Don't procrastinate (put off what should be done on-time). As a participant you must realize that it takes a certain amount of planning and work to be successful at anything worthwhile. A wise old saying states that "if a journey takes 100 steps, and you stop at 99, you might as well not have taken any steps at all." Players who show up at a festival without having taken all necessary steps toward preparation usually have an unpleasant experience. Plan ahead!

Don't wait till the last minute to select music, practice, or rehearse with your accompanist. If you are going to need an accompanist, contact that person early and make sure that they can handle the job. Don't hesitate to find someone else if you think you are being held back by poor accompanying. Your friend may play piano, but accompanying is an advanced skill. Find an experienced accompanist if at all possible. If you have a problem, let your director know right away. Don't put it off!

The Countdown

28. Select your solo or ensemble with the aid of the Band Director. Resist the strong temptation to play something at too hard a grade level. Find out what selections have proven successful for others in the past. Select your music before the Christmas holidays. Set aside time to practice during the holidays. Also, have two copies of your solo. Keep one neat and clean. Use the other one to learn from and mark as necessary. Play from the marked copy at the festival and give the clean copy to the judge. Don't forget to number the measures on both copies!

27. Ask your teacher for coaching **before** you have completely learned the piece. If your music requires an accompanist, go through the music with the accompanist at the beginning of preparation. If you are in an ensemble, get together with the other members early to get a perspective of the piece.

26. There are always specified procedures for signing up for solo and ensemble events. Be sure your director records the details of the event (i.e. title, composer, grade level, the student's name, etc.) Make certain all particulars are put down in writing...don't rely on word of mouth. It would be unfortunate to have your event entered incorrectly due to some misunderstanding. Directors should post a photocopy of the entry

form for all contestants to examine. Students look at this form to be sure your entry is correctly listed.

25. Many contests and festivals require you to number your measures. Number under the middle of each measure (This gives the judge a handy reference point when writing comments). Be sure to number the measures as soon as you get the music. Ignore repeats and D.S. or D.C. markings when numbering. Number straight through. For example, a first ending might be measures 34 and 35 and the second ending would begin with measure 36.

24. A music teacher should always coach participants. These sessions should start right after January 1st. Members of ensembles must realize that it is important not to miss practice appointments. If just one person doesn't show up the session is seriously compromised, both the playing and the morale.

23. Don't wait until the music is prepared to ask for coaching. Do just the opposite. Seek help early to avoid learning something wrong.

22. As soon as the director receives the contest or festival schedule, both the student and the director should review it. Contestants should know: a) The name of the judge, b) The location of the performance, and c) The date and time of the performance. Make sure everything is listed correctly!

21. Be sure to sign up for several coaching sessions from your music teacher. You probably won't do as well on your own. Space out the coaching sessions in the weeks before the festival to obtain the best possible results.

20. Ensure that your instrument is in top condition well in advance of the performance. Do not work on your instrument just before a performance. If work needs to be done (and this includes cleaning) do it several days ahead of schedule. This will reduce the possibility of an accident when handling the instrument at the last moment.

19. Obtain supplies (reeds, oil, etc.) well before a performance. Never perform on new reeds. Use only well-seasoned, tried-and-true reeds.

18. Perform the solo or ensemble for an "audience" prior to the performance. Schedule a special concert for parents, for a church group, or a classroom. This opportunity to play in front of an audience will serve as a "dress rehearsal" and help eliminate nervousness later when you want to do your best.

17. If at all possible avoid dropping out at the last minute. It's better to show up and play, whatever the results, than to be a "no-show." It looks very bad to see DNA (did not appear) next to your name; it is an injustice to the reputation of your band or orchestra program.

16. On the day of the festival plan to do everything well in advance; program extra time for everything -- getting up, dressing, breakfast, travel, etc.

15. Be particular about your dress. How you look makes an impression on everyone, particularly the judge. It is a good idea to dress-up a little. This shows everyone you are serious about what you're doing and that you respect the music. Remember, "people hear with their eyes!"

14. Arrive early at the festival site and take time to learn your way around. Find the warm-up room, the festival office where the results are posted, and particularly the room where you will be performing.

13. If possible, listen to a couple of events in the room where you will be playing well before you go on. This gives you a chance to size-up the room, the piano, and the judge.

12. It is very important to play with a piano that is correctly tuned to A=440. It is wise to check the pitch of the piano that you will use (using a hand-held tuner) before you perform to be sure it is "up to pitch." Don't wait until your performance time- check it early. If it is not up to pitch, you should find your director at the festival site and tell him of this problem. Some adjudicators may not take the piano's tuning into account and might criticize your intonation when the problem is actually with the piano.

11. Take time to warm-up correctly. There is usually a warm-up area provided. Avoid getting excited, don't talk a lot or be active before performing. Don't overdo on warming up.

10. Drink plenty of water before performing. Some students get dehydrated festivals.

9. Most adjudicators run ahead of schedule. At the festival keep track of your adjudicator's schedule. Be prepared to find your accompanist and play earlier. There may be schedule conflicts with your accompanist. If so, take the initiative, inform the judge, and try to work in your accompanist ahead of time. If this is not possible you may have to play at a later time. In any event, keep the judge informed.

8. Be ready to perform well in advance of your scheduled time, with your Instrument, your accompanist, and your music close at hand.

7. It is better not to eat before performing. However, eat breakfast as you normally would.

6. Hand the judge a clean copy of your selection with all measures numbered. Be sure your name, address and school name are on all of your music so it won't be lost.

5. Many adjudicators not only write comments but offer tips and instructional ideas verbally. Look forward to this special source of help. Listen carefully and respectfully.

4. Remember to pick up your music from the judge immediately after your performance.

3. Be sure to take the time to watch performances by students from other programs. You can learn much by watching and listening. Ask around and learn where some of the better players will be performing. Members of other groups will be quick to point out friends who play well.

2. Ratings should be posted within an hour after performance.

1. If you follow all of these steps, you can be confidant of an outstanding performance and a satisfying experience. To repeat the old saying mentioned earlier in this book, "if you hope to get a "superior", the result will probably be an "excellent." If you **know** you are going to get a superior, you probably will!

Good luck at festival!

• • •

Chapter 26: The "Doctor's Office" Routine For Coaching Solos and Ensembles

Student instrumentalists participating in solo and ensemble festivals must receive help from their music teachers if they are to have a positive experience playing for an adjudicator, and if they are to fully benefit from this important adjunct to the band activity. It is good for a school music program when many students participate...the more the better. It makes for stronger players, and ultimately a better band.

In many instances those players who study privately receive excellent coaching from their instructor and go on to realize "superior" results. When there are no private teachers available in the community, it falls on the director to coach the students. The Band Director's main problem however is time. How can an individual director, with a limited number of hours in the day, successfully coach a large number of students and assure them a rewarding solo and/or ensemble experience

Here is a plan I call "The Doctor's Office Routine" that can help directors coach a large number of solo and ensemble entries very efficiently. We are all familiar with the way we are handled when we go to see our doctor. First we are ushered into the examination room where we wait for the doctor. Eventually the doctor enters, examines us, and prescribes treatment. After that the nurse follows, perhaps with an injection, a knowing look, and a prescription! Why do doctors use this system for seeing patients? They use this system because it is the most efficient way to handle the largest number of patients in the shortest amount of time. The doctor can see more people and not waste his time waiting! Instead, the patients do the waiting. Band directors can adapt this same process to coaching solos and ensembles.

Here is How it Works

Set aside a specific amount of time for coaching students. For example; start three months before the event, and set aside two-hour blocks after school, or in the evenings for coaching. Designate a site with assigned coaching rooms. In a typical high school music suite this could be the chorus room, practice rooms, the instrumental rehearsal room, and maybe even nearby general classrooms.

Have the students in each event sign up weeks in advance on a master appointment calendar (chart.) This chart should list the available dates and times horizontally and the available rooms vertically. In a music suite with two practice rooms, an instrument storage room, a choral rehearsal room, an instrumental rehearsal room, and a director's office this adds up to six coaching "sites." Show these sites as six columns on the sign-up chart. Student scheduling conflicts can often be avoided if different days are offered on different weeks.

When the students arrive, they should immediately begin practicing their solos or ensembles in their assigned rooms. The director roams from room to room. When he enters each room he listens, evaluates, offers instruction and interpretation, and may work on a "tough spot" in the music. When things are going well, he leaves that room and enters the next. The students continue to practice until their assigned time is up, and then the next scheduled events arrive and the process repeats.

With this routine one director working one evening a week for two hours can coach twelve events. With students coming in once every two weeks, the director can coach twenty-four events. If the director spends three hours a week, this once-a-week scheduling allows for coaching many solo and ensemble events; quite an impressive achievement.

With this system large numbers of solo and ensemble festival entries receive adequate coaching from one director spending a minimum amount of time!

Certain problems associated with the solo and ensemble activity can prevent positive outcomes. Watch out for these pitfalls:

Word gets around quickly among band students and, if they see numerous entries dropping out, they may lose interest in solo and ensemble activities. Make sure your students are taught to honor their commitments; their solo commitments to themselves and their ensemble commitments to their friends. Also make sure that accompanists are on-hand for solo rehearsal sessions, that all registration forms are turned in on-time, and that all fees are paid. Double-check every detail.

If a program has the reputation of earning many superior ratings each year, many students will eagerly look forward to participating. Of course, the reason for such reputations is the careful planning by directors that provided adequate quality coaching and allowed the students the necessary amount of time working with accompanists and rehearsing in their ensembles.

Motivation

One very effective motivator for students is some type of personal recognition. This recognition can take the form of public announcements, medals, or plaques. Many students will want to "win a medal." Don't make the mistake of expecting all kids to participate because they are musically inspired. At first all many want to do is "win." After they mature a bit they will begin to feel the gratification that comes from musical growth. Let them enjoy winning. They will mature over time.

Accompanists

Don't expect students to be responsible for getting their own accompanists. To successfully solve the accompanist problem, the band director must assume the responsibility of procuring this service. The accompanist should be paid, and the easiest way is in the form of one check from the school or band parents association. This can be included as a line item in the band budget for the year. Students can reimburse the band parents organization if needed.

The accompanist can be included in the "Doctor's Office Routine" by being scheduled for specific times on the master schedule. In this way the same accompanist can serve several students during one session. Directors should manage this aspect of planning.

Scheduling

Nothing is more frustrating when dealing with scheduling than dealing with solo and ensemble activities. When left on their own, students are usually inept at arranging either coaching times or rehearsal times with their accompanist.

Just posting a scheduling chart and expecting every student to sign up is not going to work. The students will forget or put-off signing up. Take the chart down before every rehearsal and spend a few moments reminding the students to sign-up for coaching. Constantly remind them of their appointments, of their responsibilities, and of their commitments to one another. Be patient, but be persistent.

Initially student members of ensembles may hesitate to commit to a time or, worse, they may just not show up. When the director schedules coaching, accompanists, and enforces the obligation to show up and be responsible for commitments, the scheduling process improves. The director should announce the coaching schedule daily. Scheduling problems will not solve themselves, but they can be minimized when the director stays on top of the activity. Make it a big deal, because it is!

Performing

Players must be thoroughly coached on the entire festival process which begins when the students leave home the day of the event. It is best to "put all the eggs in one basket." By that I mean take all of the solo and ensemble students to the contest on one bus. Set the departure time early to have time to recover from students over-sleeping, forgetting, etc. This will minimize the chance of students pulling a "no show" and letting everyone else down.

• • •

PART 6:
SECRETS FOR SUCCESS IN THE BANDROOM

Chapter 27: Ensemble Seating by Challenging

The Challenge Contract as a Tool for Establishing Seating

A common method of seating members in a school ensemble is by order of ability with the best player on first chair. Other criteria for seating order may be necessary at times to meet a specific musical need, however in the school ensemble a strong incentive for students to practice and continue to develop is the lure of moving up in a section.

If seating is based only on the opinion of the director, students, administration, and parents may question the system's validity. In this proposed challenge system the seating is determined by ability in each section, the evaluation is objective and impartial, and the procedure is witnessed and documented.

This challenge system is offered complete with a set of rules and is followed by a *Challenge Contract* form which can be tailored for each school situation.

Two Dangers

1. The motivation for students to compete for top chair placement is considered by most music teachers to be a valid and ethical form of motivation; however the process can get out of hand. Challenging should be considered an exceptional event. Incessant challenging, particularly when directed toward one student, should be discouraged. Emphasis should be on the musical values and development of the ensemble, not on seating order.

2. The director must be careful to encourage healthy attitudes about winning and losing a challenge. This should not be an unpleasant

experience for the losing student. It is important that both participants leave the challenge with a positive attitude.

Rules for Challenging

1. Seat students at the beginning of the school year by seniority and only as an expediency. From this initial seating any student may challenge for any seat in the section.
2. A written contract must be taken out by a "challenger" on a "challenge." Only one challenge contract may be active at any time with any individual.
3. A losing challenger must wait two weeks before re-challenging. This allows both parties a reasonable period of time to perfect the material. It also avoids undue pressure on any one challengee from constant competition.
4. Challenges must be won by a significant margin (at least 3 points). Any score closer is considered a tie (the person being challenged retains their seat).
5. Errors to consider: a) inferior tone, b) wrong notes, c) wrong rhythms, d) incorrect dynamics, e) incorrect style, f) inferior time, etc. The director decides.
6. The challenger obtains a blank contract from the director and fills in the blanks in the presence of the challengee. All conditions must be mutually agreed upon. The director should be consulted immediately if there is a disagreement to the terms of the contract.

7. The director retains the completed contract once it is signed by both students. The director signs and dates it and keeps it on file.
8. If the challengee refuses to accept the contract, the chair is automatically relinquished to the challenger. Everyone else in the section moves according to the result. If anyone else in the section is unhappy with the new seating, they too can challenge.
9. The director should suspend all challenging for a designated period of time before major performances. This avoids last minute changes in parts assignments and allows all efforts to be directed toward mastering parts for the performance.
10. Band student officers and the director should witness challenges.
11. During the play-off the challenger goes first. The director keeps count of the errors made by both participants.
12. The director should sign the contract at the end of the play-off noting the winner, the date, and the time. Challenge contracts should be kept on file for two years.

• • •

"Name of Band"

CHALLENGE CONTRACT

We the undersigned, agree to the following challenge playoff appointment which must be established at least two weeks in advance and will be held in the band rehearsal room.

Prepared material must come from established sectional or training method books such as the Rubank Series, Arban, Klose, etc. The material must be available to all parties.

TODAY'S DATE _____

DATE OF THE CHALLENGE MUTUALLY AGREED UPON_____

TIME OF THE CHALLENGE _____

PREPARED MATERIAL_____

PAGE NUMBER _____ EXERCISE NUMBER _____

CHALLENGER'S SIGNATURE _____

CHALLENGEE'S SIGNATURE _____

CONTRACT RECEIVED DATE _____ TIME _____

DIRECTOR'S SIGNATURE _____

****

RESULTS _____

DIRECTOR'S SIGNATURE _____

DATE _____ TIME _____

Chapter 28: A Collection of Tips For Success

Success in Starting French Horn Players

Tradition dictates we start students on the single F horn, and in some band method books only fingerings for the F horn are provided. Method books are designed to favor the C and Bb instruments, not the French horn in F. For beginners playing the Horn in F the range of many method book exercises is either too high or too low. Also, all of the notes above third space C on the F horn can be played open; consequently beginners tend to miss a lot of notes. The difficulty in finding the right pitch when the partials are so close together can be quite discouraging for beginning players. This often results in a high dropout rate when beginning students start with the single F horn. As a result, the critically important beginning band, the foundation of any program, may end up with few or no horns.

Solve this problem by starting beginners on the single Bb horn instead of the F horn. Use the Horn in F method book, but write in the Bb fingerings for the students. Leave learning the F horn fingerings for later, when they move to the double horn.

Here Are Some Advantages

1. All the brasses use the same fingerings when the Bb horn player is reading Horn in F music. In other words the trumpet, baritone, tuba, and B-flat horn will use the same valve combinations.

2. Beginning notes on the Bb side are in a solid range just as they are for the other brasses. This means fewer burbles and much more confidence for the novice horn players.

3. The close partials found on the horn in F are avoided with the Bb horn. (For example the notes Bb, C, D, E, etc. can all be played open on the F horn.) The more forgiving overtone series of the Bb horn helps minimize wrong notes.

Much of the modern grade 2 literature puts the horns rather high in the close partial area on the F horn. On Bb horn the player will be able to deliver his part with much more accuracy. Usually the double French horn is one of the 'school owned' instruments furnished by the band. Middle school bands on a tight budget may want to use only single Bb horns if double horns are too expensive. Single Bb horns are the same price as single F's and much cheaper than double horns.

An Easy Way for Band Directors to Know Bb Horn Fingerings

Recall the trumpet fingering sequence from second line G down to D flat:

Bb Trumpet Fingerings from C to G

Note	Bb Fingering
G	open
Gb	2
F	1
E	12
Eb	23
D	13
Db	123

Now think of it this way; on trumpet (reading the transposed trumpet part) C, E, and G are open overtones in the staff (the second octave). On the B-flat horn (reading transposed Horn in F part) F, A, and C are open. In both cases the actual <u>concert</u> pitches for these overtones are B-flat, D, and F. The same valve combinations produce the same effect, i.e. lowering the notes by ½ steps. For example on B-flat horn F is open, E is 2nd, Eb is 1st, D Is 1st and 2nd, Db is 2nd and 3rd, etc. Here are some basic B-flat horn fingerings for reading F Horn music. Other fingerings are possible and produce slightly different tuning results. Numerous fingering charts are available online for B-flat horn. Also, see John Ericson's excellent online article for more information on this topic (Ericson, 2013).

Suggested Bb Horn Fingerings for F Horn Music

Note	Bb Fingering
G	open
Gb	2
F Top Line	open
E	2
Eb	1
D	12
Db	23
C 3rd space	open
B	2
Bb	1
A	12
Ab	23
G	1, 13
Gb	12
F 1st space	open
E	2
Eb	1

A word of caution: Do not use Horn in Bb sheet music that is found in some marching arrangements. Use ONLY Horn in F music and teach the students their Bb fingerings, then they will be ready for the concert music and eventually the double horn.

By the way, some argue that the bell front marching Bb French horns seem to have a little better intonation. Another good reason for getting on the Bb horn kick!

A Tool to Pull Stuck Swabs

Beginning clarinet players sometimes get their swabs stuck inside their instruments. The more they try to remove the swab by poking it out, the tighter it gets stuck. Warn them about this hazard, and ask them to come to you with the problem because you have a special invention that will remove the swab with ease and without damaging the clarinet.

Make This Tool for Stuck Swabs:

- Weld a medium sized machine screw to a welding rod about 14 inches long. Bend the other end back 3 inches to form a handle.

- To remove a stuck swab, screw the tool into the stuck swab and slowly pull. The bunched up swab will gradually loosen, and it can be pulled out of the instrument.

Warning: Remember to warn students ahead of time not to force a stuck swab. Have them bring it to you, because you have a tool that will pull it out without damaging the instrument.

The Mystery of the Squeaking Clarinets Part 2

This is a more detailed review of the problem I outlined in Chapter 9 concerning clarinet and sax players beginning to squeak after they had been playing a few years. In my experience they seemed to develop this problem over time and hadn't had it earlier in beginning bend. Why?

This is what I learned from the well-known clinician Nilo Hovey when he spent a week at the University of Miami Band Camp where I was an instructor. Beginner model clarinets usually come with mouthpieces that are made of molded plastic. In the molding process the material is put under heavy compression. After molding, the facing is machined onto the mouthpiece. Over a period of time, usually about three years, the plastic begins to expand back to its original state. This causes the table of the mouthpiece to begin to warp slightly, and this warped table causes reeds to squeak. Attempts can be made to reface the mouthpiece...after all; the mouthpiece isn't any good as is. However, a lot of skill is needed to do this.

The best solution is to convince the servicing music dealer to include a hard rubber, professional quality mouthpiece (of your selection) in the initial rental or sale. Ultimately this will be the most economical solution for the student.

For students who already have a squeaking mouthpiece, explain to them what has happened and have them buy a new, high quality hard rubber mouthpiece.

Laminate Favorite Sheet Music

Laminate favorite warm up routines, parts to the school fight song and alma mater, the national anthem, etc.. Laminating sheet music parts greatly extends their life and utility.

Requiring Practice Schedules

Requiring practice sheets is a matter of personal preference. However, I found using parent signed practice schedules to be counter-productive. Here's why: It tempts parents and students to lie and claim more time so the child will get a better grade in band. Processing numerous practice forms is another time consuming chore for already overburdened band directors. Keeping up with these forms is a nuisance. In my view a better solution is to get the band students into the habit of taking their instruments home for practice every day.

Playing Tests

I suggest a limited number of playing tests after the first year (Beginning Band). Playing tests are good motivators when used in moderation...just don't overdo it. After all, students almost always join band to "have fun." The most important attitude for the band director to establish is that it's fun to play in the band. Once the students decide that "band is fun" it becomes the most special activity in their school day. Once the right attitude is in place, little needs to be said about requiring practice or anything else. The students will just see that the job is done because they like band so much!

The "Do It Again" Rule

Many times the quickest way to fix something in rehearsal is simply to give the ensemble an opportunity to play it again. Try this technique; tell the students that when you stop to give feedback and then immediately start conducting again (without saying where) you want them to repeat the same section. This technique saves much rehearsal time and eliminates unnecessary talking.

For example: You might start at letter 'D', play for a while and then decide to play the section again. Simply cut the band off, give your feedback, and then start conducting again without saying anything. To the group this means "Go back to wherever you started before and DO IT AGAIN." In this case, "Start at letter 'D' again." This technique is a valuable time saver. Many times the quickest and best way to improve the group's performance is to say nothing and just play it again. How many times do you remember when one of your teachers wasted time by talking? Talk less, play more.

Mark Parts Beforehand

Before handing out a selection, look over the score and mark the spots that you think may cause trouble. Then look at the individual parts and mark them too. After several rehearsals, go through the same process again. The second time through the process you will probably identify just about every single trouble spot. Then in subsequent rehearsals, concentrate on just the trouble spots. While somewhat time consuming initially, marking the score and parts actually saves a lot of time later.

A Visual Way to Teach Dynamics

This technique gives students a visual and physical picture of the relative power of the dynamic spectrum. It lets them feel and hear how each dynamic relates to the others. First, draw this chart on the board:

Range of Air and Dynamics

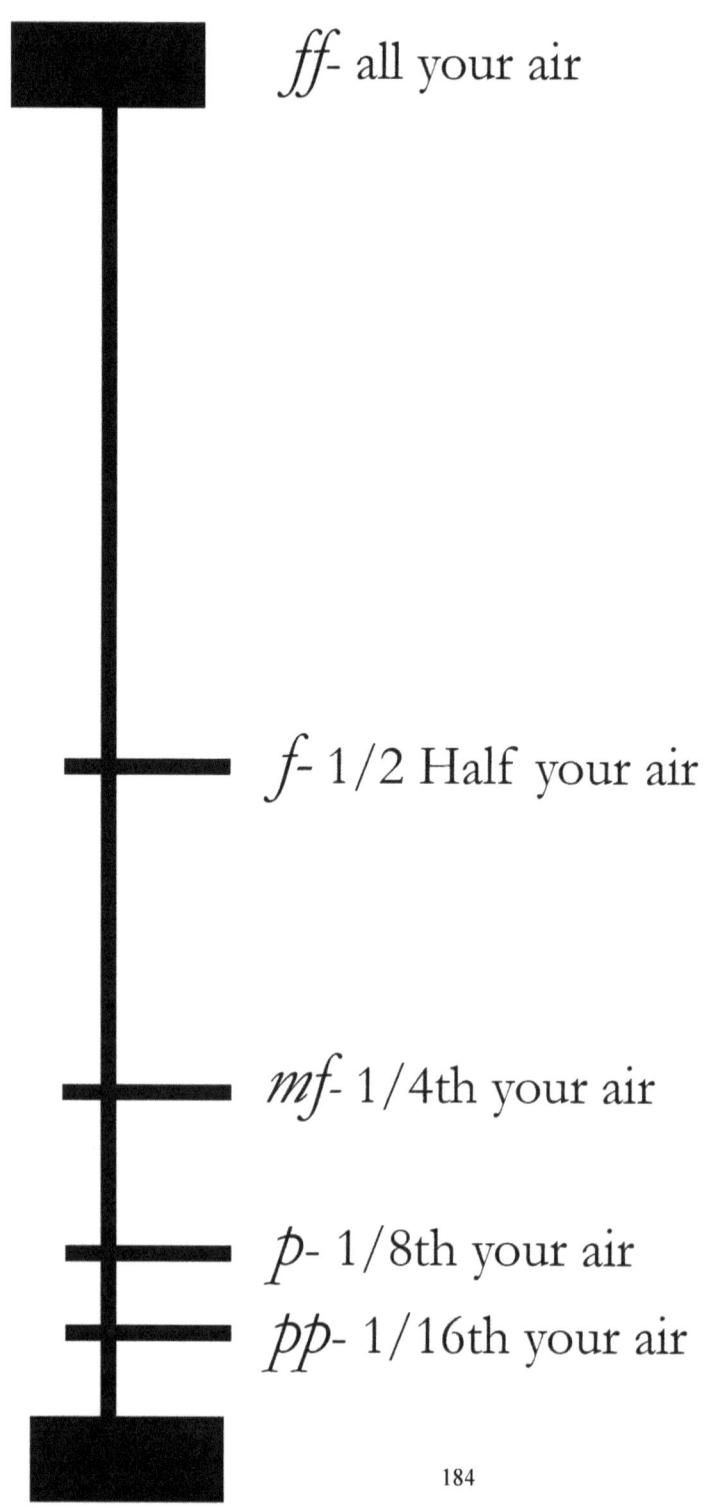

For added emphasis you can point with your baton to the various lengths (full, half, 1/4, 1/8, and 1/16) to show them the relative amount of air it takes to play these five basic dynamics.

Next, have the band play various dynamics on a unison or chord while you point to where they fall on the chart. This allows every player to **visualize** the relationship, to physically **feel** how much air it takes for each dynamic, and to **hear** what the band sounds like at each level.

After the group becomes somewhat proficient, warn them against the most common mistakes (and practice to overcome them). They are:

1. Be sure to reach a full *ff* (all the air) and avoid the point half way between *f* and *ff*.

2. Be sure *mf* is 1/4 air and no louder.

3. *p* at 1/8 air and *pp* at 1/16 air are the hardest. Practice for precision of attack and exact air. This means concentrating on breath support, projection, and "fast" air.

When you notice that ensemble dynamics are out of balance during a rehearsal, you can quickly run through this little drill to remind the students of how the dynamics relate to one another.

Mutes Change Pitch

Brass players should be taught that mutes change the pitch of the instrument. For good intonation during an extended or delicate muted passage compensate by a quick tuning slide adjustment. Don't forget to put the slide back when the mute comes out.

Straight mutes sharpen the pitch of trumpets and trombones, so pull the tuning slide slightly. Cup Mutes flatten the pitch, so push in.

"Tut" Is Bad

Tell your students that there are two teams: 1) the reeds and 2) everyone else. Reed players may put their tongue back to stop a tone. Everyone else does not. Team 2: Don't say "TUT TUT." This is one of the glaring and very common bad habits that creep into a band. It's easy to use the tongue to stop a tone on trumpet, flute, etc. Students must be taught to say "DAH DAH" stopping the tone with "ah." ALL Attacks Must Be DA. Tell students, "We're a DADA band and not a TUT TUT band."

Executing a Balanced Crescendo and Diminuendo

If we allow all players in the band to crescendo and decrescendo with everyone increasing and decreasing the volume together, the effect will not be balanced.

For a balanced crescendo the bass instruments should start to get louder first, then the middle voices execute the regular pattern, and finally the treble instruments wait to be the last group to start the crescendo. Like this:

Balanced Crescendo:

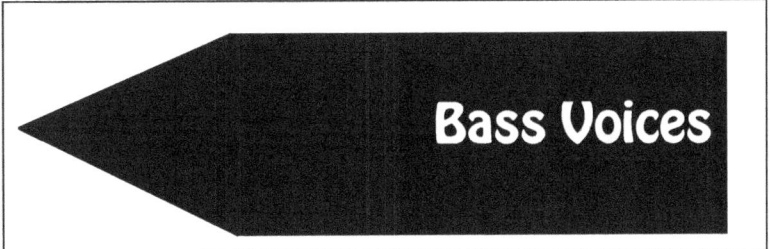

For a balanced diminuendo, reverse the process:

Balanced Diminuendo:

. . .

Chapter 29: Medical Treatment Permission

During a trip an accident may occur which requires a band member to receive medical attention. Hospitals have been known to delay treating students until legal permission is obtained from the parents. There have been times when students have been forced to wait in pain until hospital administrators contact their parents or guardians. To avoid needless delays in students getting treatment, I suggest the following procedures.

Consult with your school system's legal representatives and develop a form that will allow for medical treatment for your students. This form should address among other things, permission for emergency medical treatment, allergies, special medical problems, family physician and address, and insurance details. At the beginning of the school year send this form home to the parents (or guardians) of each band member. Require each band member to have this form on file before being eligible to travel as a member of the band. Emphasize to your students this form must contain the notarized signature of their parent or legal guardian.

Keep these original forms in a three-ring notebook cover. Take this "book" on every band trip. Make sure the "book" accompanies students when they are brought to an emergency room so treatment won't be delayed.

. . .

Chapter 30: Personal Philosophy

"Music students learn more than music- they learn of life and self-worth. You are a valuable person in the lives of your students. "Don't underestimate the importance of your work or the responsibility that your job demands; enjoy it."

--Nilo Hovey

The Danger of Having Views

When expressing my views, I realize that I open myself up to criticism, but that's better than keeping quiet. Why? Because out of the ensuing discussions will come a few "gems." In recent years I feel band directors have been "clamming up." This is not good.

Three years ago both the south and central state festivals were in Lakeland. I sat through six days and heard almost every band. It became obvious that most band directors were quite dedicated and went far beyond the call of duty. I am glad that I finally have the chance to say that publically.

Support One Another and Our Profession

It used to be "the thing to do" to fill the auditorium at state festival in the afternoons and hear the "big" bands." These performances were great triumphs. Today the auditorium is mostly empty. This is a serious mistake. It is important for both the band director and the students to hear the best programs in the state. Plan to stay. Don't leave early!

In the past when I have done clinics, guest conducting, and judging gigs I have asked kids, "Have you ever heard a live band concert?" Many have answered "NO!" How can they develop a discriminating ear? When asked to play with a fine tone, how do they know what it sounds like if they haven't heard examples of fine tones? Make the extra effort to arrange for your band to stay and listen to other bands. It is worth it!

Don't Make Rash Decisions

Develop an aversion to this. A rash motion could pass from the floor to change something. This is dangerous! The safer way is to refer the motion to a committee for examination and not take immediate action. Sometimes the reasons for existing policies are not readily apparent to the general membership (especially the less experienced members). There is not enough time allowed for discussions at the state clinic in January. The ideal time to propose changes is during the summer convention, not the All-State clinic.

Festival Ideas

The band festival system is a very useful tool. Actually, it is a wonderful tool. It makes the band director accountable and forces him/her to focus on doing a good job. What other classes or activities in school, outside sports and the arts, publically exhibit for critical evaluation the quality of instruction?

Judging is remarkably accurate when considering the thousands of "calls" that are made every year. Sure, now-and-then there is a bad call, but this is seldom the case. And what director is happy with a low rating? Festival ratings gain the attention of parents, administrators, and the directors. Sometimes low ratings motivate harder, better quality work. Caution: Ratings need to be kept in perspective, especially with young directors. This is where mentors can really help.

What is the hallmark of a top quality band director? All "superiors" at State Festival.

Marching Band

I operated the Lakeland band under limited marching band (MB) parameters. Most of the Lakeland kids didn't like marching and I was Luke-warm. We had MB rehearsal one night a week and did not do MB contests (although I am not anti-contest.) We did work, however, to get a superior rating at the FBA district marching festival. I used MB season to develop playing fundamentals, particularly SONORITY.

We started a dance corps, and later a flag corps, so the band could stand and play most of the time at football games. The audience saw a new dance routine each game. I just gave the dance team sponsor a tape one month ahead so the members could learn the dance routines and be ready to go.

My philosophy on MB fundamentals was the same as playing - develop strong MB fundamentals.

I never made it as a show designer. I went to Bands of America clinics for three years straight and attended clinics by many of the big-name designers. I died a thousand deaths trying to design. But I finally figured it out. Learning to arrange by doing one tune a year is a bad idea. Learning to design by doing one show a year is equally bad. Those who do twenty or more shows a year for many years get really good at it. So buy your show from one of the experts!

I learned a lot by watching Rob Roadman and Tom Bishop's marching bands over the years. They both used relatively simple drill designs, but had super clean execution – both playing and marching.

My Recommendation: For a high quality MB show, buy your show from an expert, keep it simple, and clean, clean, clean.

• • •

Chapter 31: More Tips on Becoming a Better Band Director

Get Out of Town

There is a danger in becoming "marooned" in your own band room. Find activities beyond your own back yard. Attend events like Bands of America, Atlanta Band and Orchestra Conference, the Mid-West Clinic, DCI, etc. Develop exchange concerts with colleague/friend in a similar school. Caution: Plan ahead and stay in a motel, not in student's homes.

Utilize the FBA and NETWORK. Communication among Band directors is very important. Don't clam-up.

When I was in Auburndale, Tom Bishop was in Lake Wales and we both had class B bands. In those days (1960s) getting out of town was difficult. We found that one secret was to get several kids to band camp for 5 weeks every summer. When they returned they "infected" the other members with what they had learned.

In recent years band camps have become much shorter, largely due to cost per student. We still need four to five week camps. Is there a way for FBA to work with universities and start a 4-week camp with a staff of high school/middle school BDs, not university people? Let's do it like McCall did it at Miami!

The Thing To Do

Today many band directors whine and wring their hands. "The kids have so much to do. It's hard to motivate them. It's hard to schedule." Wrong! Band directors need to get busy and figure out how to make such a dynamic and important program that the kids won't dare miss it. Make your band "THE THING TO DO" in your school. Success breeds success. Success motivates.

Fundamentals

Building strong fundamentals is like building a savings account.

1. It is a problem having a band that is "on the line" between a I or a II. Solution: Elmer Magnell at FSU used to say a strong section will bring everyone else along.
2. Buttonhole promising talent in middle school and get them started with private lessons and band camp. A strong high school program must have a strong feeder program.
3. You must work your concert band from day one. If you wait until the end of marching season, you will never make it.
4. Kids have trouble finding appropriate band recordings. Provide them with suggestions for what to look for and where to look.
5. Suggest specific recordings for your jazz band students. I found that almost all of my kids had never heard a jazz band! How can they know how they are supposed to sound if they don't have a reference?
6. Build a firm foundation of both marching and musical fundamentals.
7. Teach by routines, and avoid teaching by rote.
8. Provide opportunities for kids to hear and see other bands.
9. Do at least 5 one-hour concerts per year to develop the performance routine.
10. Concentrate on fine sonority all the time.

The Listening Festival Idea

Hold this festival several weeks prior to District Festival. Invite five bands. Rule: All must be in audience by 9:00 A.M. and listen to everyone else. The host college band is last on the program. I think Stetson and UF are already doing this?

Band Literature Yesterday and Today

In Fillmore's day "common practice harmony" was the norm and was common in transcriptions of overtures, waltzes, novelties, and intermezzos. Original band compositions were limited in scope.

In old scoring everyone played all the time (much doubling). In modern band compositions there is much more variety in texture and color, thinner scoring, and the brass only plays about one-half the time.

In community band I notice no stopping with the Warren Barker arrangements. There are more frequent stops with older literature. Why? Everyone is playing all the time.

Regarding the modern trend of rearranging old masterpieces; why do arrangers do this? They take pieces from public domain, change a few things, and then get full royalties. This is bad! Besides, with some things, like Souse marches, they ruin the original intent! I recommend that we honor original arrangements as much as possible.

Today there seems to be confusion in interpreting marches. Should we stylize marches? I say it becomes a question of being authentic. Find recordings of Sousa's band do it like he did it! Check out the Air Force Reserve Band's Fillmore CD (*Military Escort*). That's how Henry did it!

Today I believe we are in danger of losing our audience (and our support base) by performing too much esoteric music, yet we want to push back the frontier and exploit the best in contemporary literature. We must solve this problem or lose audiences and eventually lose the entire program. Consider your audience. Festival judges and audiences will appreciate Husa. Grandma won't. Program different, lighter selections for your public concerts.

My philosophy in music selection is to program romantic, not baroque or classical. Why? Romantic and neo-romantic music offers more compositional devices, and better displays the band. Examples: rubato, soaring melodies, contoured phrasing, more varied color and texture scoring.

Music out of print -- Is anything being done to make it possible to recover band music that is out of print? We (FBA) should encourage publishers to make out-of-print music available once again using new technologies like electronically scanned pdf versions.

The "Thing To Do" or "Not The Thing To Do"

Many of our activities can be looked upon this way. It's the thing to do to take one's bands to festival. Years ago a band director never had someone visit. Today it's more common to hear, "Would you come work my band." This is a very good "thing to do."

In our area (Central Florida) the thing is to be friendly with other Band directors. In some areas band directors don't seem to get along as well. However in our area it is "not the thing to do" to encourage kids to go to concerts of others. Bad! Members of the military bands that tour our state say this varies from one area to another.

• • •

PART 7:

RETROSPECTIVE

Chapter 32: My Recollections of Henry Fillmore
From Sept. 1952 until his death Dec. 7, 1956

A Few Stories about Henry Before I Knew Him

Henry was very proud of a grandfather clock that was prominently displayed in his house. He had dedicated his march "Golden Friendships" to the members of Syrian Temple Shrine Band from Cincinnati, and the clock was a gift (in 1926) from that band.

He would often have entire bands stop by his house. When Dick Bowles was with the Lafayette H.S. Band they came down for the Orange Bowl. Henry had them stop by and Gus Perry was the band's guide. The kids stripped Henry's little orange grove of almost all of the fruit!

Mike the Radio Dog -- Henry taught Mike to bark on cue during radio broadcasts. He brought Mike to the ABA Convention and some members made a "scene" about Henry keeping Mike in the room. Henry kept him anyway. The picture from the convention shows the ABA top brass, Fillmore, and Mike. Henry said "some of the guys took themselves too seriously."

During the Miami Band's trip to El Salvador, I think it was around January of 1954; Henry gave many of the guys in the band a dollar and asked them to buy an extra bottle of tequila (so Henry could avoid the import tariff). At the Airport he pulled his Lincoln convertible out front and the guys filled up the trunk with bottles. Later at his house he greeted us with a candle lit ceremony in his kitchen where he opened all of his cabinet doors, revealing dozens of shimmering bottles of tequila. Mable would never have allowed this. When he drank a little too much Mable would warn "Henry, you're glowing."

On their wedding anniversary each year, Henry and Mable would eat alone. They would have a can of baked beans by the light of one candle, remembering when they had very little.

When I Knew Him

He would drive his white Lincoln convertible up next to the drill field and the Hurricanettes would run over and hug him. Everything stopped while we watched.

He watched the football practices so much that the team made him an honorary coach or manager or something. He loved to talk football and was especially fond of baseball.

Every other year the U. of M. Band would travel via train to Gainesville for the football game between the Hurricanes and the Gators. Busses would take the band to the student union where they would attend a banquet with the Gator Band. Henry would present his extremely entertaining "one man opera." Forty years later at an FMEA Clinic, I was having an afternoon snack at Tampa Convention center with Gus Perry and Reid Poole. I mentioned the banquets and Poole informed me that Henry had paid for it all!

The Miami band would sometimes play ballyhoo music for fund raisers around Miami. There was always a buffet for the band "down the hall." I have since learned that Henry paid for all that too.

Henry loved to treat.

On many of our frequent trips to his house on Friday and Saturday nights he would say "let's go get a hamburger." We would usually end up at a fancy restaurant instead where he loved to say "top of the menu boys, it's all on me." We would then go back to his house and listen to stories until 4 A.M.

The Orange Bowl Parade: The Miami bands always lead the parade (Playing *Orange Bowl* march, of course.) Henry would have a student drive him in his Lincoln convertible, with signs on the side, just behind the band. He would have Fred McCall (U of M band director) ride with him. In front of the reviewing stand he would get out and go up to his reserved seat.

In 1954 the start of the Orange Bowl parade was delayed for some reason and I asked to go talk to August Schaffer who was with the Shrine Band behind us on the street. I asked him about his ideas for interpretation of *Willow Echoes*. Two weeks later he died.

As Henry got older his tempos got faster. He flew through the marches and smears. Everything dot faster except the novelty numbers.

Marches were his greatest works and his transcriptions were classics! On the other hand, his novelty numbers were quite corny.

The University of Miami Band Camps

The student rooms in the camps were organized into a cabin system. Henry had his room designated as "Cabin Zero." Every day the cabin leaders reported attendance at the evening meetings. Henry would stand and report "all present and accounted for from Cabin Zero." This always got a big laugh.

Henry had asthma and he had an A/C unit put in his dorm room. The U. of M. said nothing!

Henry worked for the U. of M. for a $1.00 per year!

His music was kept permanently in folios at U.M., Coral Gables, and Miami High.

The President's March was written for Henry King Stanford, President of the U. of M.

Sometimes when Henry needed a ride I would take him. Once we got to listening to a Cincinnati Reds ball game on the radio. We sat in the car until the end of the game and ran the battery down. We got a jump easily.

During band camp the code name for a party in his room was "lodge meeting tonight." The parties continued after his death. Otto (Kraushaar) and (Fred) McCall never attended. But Tom Bishop, Bill Higgins, Bill Bennett, Larry Trembley, Paul Yoder, Harry Grant, Bill Russell, and I did!

Each year Yoder and Rosie (wife) would do a standup routine that had us on the floor. Yoder said he would always thank college and service bands he guest conducted when they wouldn't give him a hard time.

Henry threw party for Phi Mu Alpha each year. He called it the Banquet at Henre's. Only special faculty were invited; Dr. Collins, Larry Trembley. McCall was NOT there. Henry decorated the room with beer steins. On time Trembley challenged the Dean to "chug a lug." Each took down a stein. The Dean left soon thereafter.

Henry always enjoyed life's simple pleasures and one of his favorites was to feed, and talk to, the ducks. Glenn Cliff Bainum, from the Northwestern University band, got a real charge out Henry talking to the ducks when he visited.

After the banquet, and the annual performance of Tom Bishop's special arrangement of the Finale to "Symphony number 4" at the end of the summer band camp one year Henry called me, Bill Clark, and Bill Higgins aside and said "I have a problem." He had a bunch of beer cans in plastic bags he wanted us to discreetly throw away. We drove all over Coral Gables and finally ended up behind a grocery in South Miami.

Miami Band Tours

For me the most fun we had in the UM Band was on tour. One year Harold Supank had a piccolo solo and one night Henry brought a marble egg and some Spanish moss and had it placed on Harold's chair while he was out front. Harold jumped up thinking he had sat on his flute. Henry picked up the egg, and said, "Oh, I think Harold laid an egg."

Another time Henry had the busses stop at his sister Mary's house in Vero Beach. He then proceeded to have entire band walk through the house.

Henry said you must have two levels, district and state, to have real quality. Dick Bowles also told me this. Henry said about a third of the band needed to get superior ratings at solo and ensemble festival in order for a program to really grow. He further believed that judging should always be undertaken in a manner that encouraged growth and promoted bands.

Henry's conducting trick to pick up a sagging tempo was to snap the baton like a buggy whip.

Henry was a good friend of Paul Lavalle, director of the Band of America. In 1953 he got Lavalle to do a guest appearance with the UM Band. We were on NBC radio and this was before TV. Lavalle in turn had Henry take the Band of America program for a week. This was truly big time stuff.

For some reason Edwin Franco Goldman blocked Lavalle from getting into ABA. It may have had something to do with a meeting between Lavalle, Henry, and Goldman at a Fordham football game.

One year for the Orange Bowl halftime show Henry used a bunch of palm trees as props. But he made no arrangements to dispose of them.

Henry died on December 7, 1956, a Friday night. A number of band directors met at U. of F. band room on Sunday the 9th to hear the Gator Band read all of the new required numbers for FBA festival performance. As usual everyone brought tape recorders and the band provided a long extension snake for everyone to plug into. Colonel Bachman took the podium to announce Henry's death, broke down, and had to leave the room. The president of FBA started the band on Military Escort and left an empty podium. There was not a dry eye in the place.

• • •

Bibliography

Bachman, H. B. (1965). Styling of Standard Marches (Lecture). University of Florida.

Byo, J. L., Schlegel, A. L., & Clark, N. A. (2011). Effects of Stimulus Octave and Timbre on the Tuning Accuracy of Secondary School Instrumentalists. *Journal of Research in Music Education, 58*(4), 316–328.

Clark, N. A. (2012). *Direction of Mistuning, Magnitude of Cent Deviation, and Timbre as Factors in Musicians' Pitch Discrimination in Simultaneous and Sequential Listening Conditions.* (Unpublished doctoral dissertation). Louisiana State University, Louisiana.

Clark, N. A. (2008). Rekindling the Culture of Mentorship, *NBA Journal 48*(3), 17.

Deffayet, Daniel (Posted 2009). Mussorgsky's *Pictures at an Exhibition.* Retrieved from http://www.youtube.com/watch?v=LLkm1G93NEU

Deming, W. Edwards (1986). *Out of the Crisis.* Cambridge, MA: MIT Press.

Duke, R. A. (2007). *Intelligent Music Teaching: Essays on the Core Principles of Effective Instruction.* Austin, Texas: Learning and Behavior Resources.

Duke, R. A. (1985). Wind instrumentalists' Intonational Performance of Selected Musical Intervals. *Journal of Research in Music Education, 33*(2), 101-111.

Duke, R. A., Geringer, J. M., & Madsen, C. K. (1988). Effect of Tempo on Pitch Perception. *Journal of Research in Music Education, 36*(2), 108-125.

Ericson, John. *Getting Started on the Horn.* Arizona State University Webpage. http://www.public.asu.edu/~jqerics/beginners.html (Accessed June 17, 2013).

Ericsson, K. A., Krampe, R. T., & Tesch-Römer, C. (1993). The Role of Deliberate Practice in the Acquisition of Expert Performance. *Psychological review, 100*(3), 363.

Franch-Ballester, Jose (Posted 2012). *Backun Clarinet Concepts | Tongue Positioning with Jose Franch-Ballester.*
http://www.youtube.com/watch?v=Cz6lencLOGQ

Fussell, Raymond C. (1985). *Exercises for Ensemble Drill.* Los Angeles: Alfred Publishing Company, Inc.

Fyk, J. (1987). Duration of tones required for satisfactory precision of pitch matching. *Bulletin of the Council for Research in Music Education, 91,* 38-44.

Garrison, C., Ehringhaus, M. (2008). Formative and Summative Assessments in the Classroom.
http://ccti.colfihttp://ccti.colfinder.org/sites/default/files/formative_and_summative_assessment_in_the_classroom.pdf. (Accessed July 2008, June 2014).

Geringer, J. M., & Witt, A. C. (1985). An Investigation of Tuning Performance and Perception of String Instrumentalists. *Bulletin of the Council for Research in Music Education, 85,* 90-101.

Hovey, Nilo (ca. 1950). *Section Studies for Bb Clarinets.* New York: Belwin, Inc. (Out of print)

Livingston, J. S. (1969). Pygmalion in Management: A Manager's Expectations are the Key to a Subordinate's Performance and Development. *Harvard Business Review, 47*(4).

Lussy, M. (1892, 1952). *Musical Expression: Accents, Nuances, and Tempo, in Vocal and Instrumental Music* (Vol. 25). Novello, Ewer and co., H. W. Gray Co. agents for USA

Madsen, C. K., Edmonson, F. A., & Madsen, C. K. (1969). Modulated Frequency Discrimination in Relationship to Age and Musical Training. *Journal of the Acoustical Society of America, 46*(6), 1468-1472.

McBeth, W. F. (1972). *Effective Performance of Band Music.* San Antonio, TX: Southern Music.

Menza, Don (Posted 2010). *Don Menza - Lesson on Tone - Cannonball Saxophones.* http://www.youtube.com/watch?v=5Oc0VzGBPxY

Mercer, R. J. (1970). *The Band Director's Brain Bank.* Evanston, IL: Instrumentalist Company.

Miles, E. M. (1972). Beat Elimination as a Means of Teaching Intonation to Beginning Wind Instrumentalists. *Journal of Research in Music Education, 20*(4), 496-500.

Platt, J. R., & Racine, R. J. (1985). Effect of Frequency, Timbre, Experience, and Feedback on Musical Tuning Skills. *Perception and Psychophysics, 38,* 543–553.

Pottle, Ralph R. (1966). *Tuning the School Band and Orchestra.* Hammond, Louisiana: Ralph R. Pottle.

Righter, Charles B. (1955). *Success in Teaching: School Orchestras and Bands.* Minneapolis, MN: Paul A. Schmitt Music Company.

Smith, Leonard B. (1980). *Treasury of Scales.* Miami, FL: Belwin, Inc.

Stauffer, Donald (1987). *Intonation Deficiencies of Wind Instruments in Ensemble.* Birmingham, AL: Stauffer Press.

Sueta, Ed, (1985). *Rhythm Vocabulary Charts for Effective Rhythmic Development- Book 1.* Voorhees, NJ: Charles Dumont & Son, Inc.

VanderCook, H. A. (1942). *Expression in Music.* Chicago, IL: Rubank. (Revised and published by Rubank Publishing in 1989)

Wheeler, R. L. (Posted, 2010). *Ray Wheeler Clarinet & Tongue.* http://www.youtube.com/watch?v=Id5O3Tk5YV8

Wheeler, R. L. (1973). Tongue Registration and Articulation for Single and Double Reed *National Association of College Wind and Percussion Instructors XXII* (2), 3-12.

Wickes, F. B. (1990). The Strobe: a Forgotten Friend. *Flute Talk.* September, 20-21.

Wooden, J. R., Tobin, J., & Walton, B. (1988). *They Call Me Coach*. Chicago, IL: Contemporary Books.

Worthy, M. D. (2000). Effects of Tone-Quality Conditions on Perception and Performance of Pitch Among Selected Wind Instrumentalists. *Journal of Research in Music Education, 48*(3), 222-236.

Voxman, H., & Gower, W. (1954). *Rubank Advanced Method, [Various Instruments]*. Chicago, IL: Rubank Publications. (Republished in 1992.)

CD Recordings

Alexander, R., Bagley, E.E., Elliott, Z., Sousa, J.P. (1700-). *ON PARADE--World's Greatest Marches* [Music C.D.] [Recorded by The University of Michigan Symphonic Band and The University of Michigan Symphonic Band.]. Quintessence.

Allen, E. W. Sounds of John Philip Sousa -- Authentic Rehearsal Techniques for the Preparation and *Interpretation of Recorded Marches*. The United States Army Band. This CD and an extensive booklet were available from the American School Band Directors Association (ASBDA). Membership in ASBDA was not required for purchase.

Henry Fillmore. (1881-1956). *Military Escort: The Music of Henry Fillmore* [Music C.D.]. Warner Robins, GA: [Recorded by The Band of the United States Air Force Reserve.] [Director: Clark, N.A.; Producer: Miller, W.C.] This CD is available through Amazon.com

Sousa, J.P. (1888). Semper Fidelis [Recorded by The United States Marine Band]. On *Music of John Philip Sousa* [Music C.D.]. Washington D.C.: The United States Marine Band. (2009).

• • •

Biographies

William Clayton Miller earned degrees in music education from the University of Miami, Coral Gables, Florida, and Florida State University. He taught instrumental music in florida for thirty four years and remained active as a band adjudicator, clinician, and guest conductor throughout his retirement. Mr. Miller spent 12 years early in his teaching career as band director in Auburndale, Florida where he taught students in grades six through twelve. After three years of doctoral studies at the University of Miami where he studied with Clifton Williams and Alfred Reed, he returned to Central Florida as band director at Lakeland Senior High School, Lakeland, Florida. He was on the staff of the five-week long Summer Music Camps at the University of Miami and Webber College for a total of twenty years. During his tenure at Lakeland High, the band was invited to the University of Florida's Festival of Winds. Numerous times the jazz band performed at the University of Florida Jazz Festival and in 1978 the Lakeland Symphonic Band was invited to perform at the National Band Association convention in Knoxville, TN. In 1979 LHS gave a concert performance for the general meeting at the All-State Florida Music Educators Association in Tampa, Florida.

Dr. N. Alan Clark is currently Director of Bands at Middle Georgia State College. He has taught and conducted at all levels from middle school through high school to professional military bands. While teaching high school in Lakeland, Florida he also served as an adjunct music faculty member at Florida Southern College and as an instructor with the Suncoast Sound Drum and Bugle Corps. In 1978 he entered the US Air Force and served as saxophone section leader and Assistant Drum Major of the Air Force Band of the West in San Antonio, Texas. In 1990 he was commissioned as an Air Force Band Officer and appointed Deputy Commander of the Band of the United States Air Forces in Europe. He also served as Deputy Commander of the Air Force Band of Flight in Dayton, Ohio and as a rehearsal conductor of the Miami Valley Symphony Orchestra. In 1996 he assumed his last conducting command with The Band of the United States Air Force Reserve in Warner Robins, Georgia. He is currently

NBA's Jazz Activities Chair and is also a member of NAfME, CBDNA, Pi Kappa Lambda, Kappa Kappa Psi, and Phi Mu Alpha. Clark holds both the Bachelor of Music Education and Master of Fine Arts in Saxophone Performance degrees from the University of Florida, as well as Master of Science in International Relations from Troy University. He received his PhD in Music Education with a minor in composition from Louisiana State University in 2012.

• • •

www.ingramcontent.com/pod-product-compliance
Lightning Source LLC
Chambersburg PA
CBHW080541170426

43195CB00016B/2635